Praise for *Strategy-In-Action*

"*Strategy-In-Action* brings the really granular current thinking of how strategy needs to be constantly measured, monitored and pivoted upon. The insights will force you to think and then rethink what you thought you knew."
—MALCOLM ELVEY, Chairman, Academy of Chief Executives

"Most of my work happens at the intersection of medicine, public health and business, so strategy and stakeholder management are my daily bread and butter. *Strategy-In-Action* allows us to make strategy in a way that doesn't just end up in a dusty filing cabinet, but mobilizes all relevant stakeholders, leads to coordinated actions and ensures targeted outcomes. This indispensable book will transform the way you think and act strategically."
—Prof. Dr. Thomas D. Szucs, Chairman of the Board, Helsana; Director, European Center for Pharmaceutical Medicine, University of Basel

"*Strategy-In-Action* is super. You present this complex process really simply and in a way that matches fully my experience. The examples are great and you bring enormous experience. The book is brilliant and has brought me much inspiration."
—STEFAN HANGARTNER, Board of Directors, Tarat SA

"*Strategy-In-Action* is highly systematic, but still manages to keep the human element at the core of strategy. It has helped us to unify our leadership team around one vision and one strategy. I strongly recommend this very helpful and worthwhile book to any CEO who needs to build alignment and an actionable strategy that mobilizes people across the company. Read *Strategy-In-Action*. Then build and execute the future you want."
—STEVEN ESSES, CEO, Arotech

"Thomas and Ed's excellent book provides 21st-century thinking and a holistic approach to the design and execution of the strategic process. Seven simple steps guide you through Strategy-In-Action to yield sustainable success. Love how it 'marries' the importance of design, implementation, and PEOPLE as critical to making it all happen."
—LISA GRATTAN, Member, Board of Directors, Women's Tennis Association

"I was highly skeptical in the beginning—I am known as a skeptical guy—but now I wish I had had your tools 35 years ago when I was starting out. Strategy-In-Action gives you everything you always wanted to know about strategy but were afraid to ask. The book distills all the complexities of strategic design and action into a simple 7-step process you and your people can actually manage and align around. Believe me, I have tried it and it works. You can get to the future your company needs and you want."
—WERNER BRANDMAYR, former President & Managing Director, ConocoPhillips Holding Europe

"(The authors) are constantly innovating (their) approach to strategic planning. They integrate the many components of a strategy into an understandable, living process, shared by the team members, with great value and applicability and which generates more than the desired results."
—HUGO CARDONA, President, SER National

"The methodology is great and the experience from working with other companies stimulating. I see measurable results in the organization: more (and more open) communication across managers and employees, better alignment across silos, and deeper ownership of the strategy. All three are essential for success."
—DR. MARIO CRAMERI, CIO Switzerland, Credit Suisse

"I have personally experienced the power of the *Strategy-In-Action* methodology. We developed a shared understanding around obstacles, breakdowns and objectives. We identified immediate action steps that optimized our de-

ployment and designed energizing 100-day 'Catalytic Projects.' *Strategy-in-Action* provides insight into how to recognize and identify traps (such as the illusion of hope and the attachment to old solutions) as well as a formula for vision and action. The adrenalin is pumping again, and we have results that were virtually impossible before *Strategy-In-Action*."
—LAWRENCE OBSTFELD, CEO, Image Navigation

"*Strategy-In-Action* offers readers a systematic, almost foolproof methodology for building the company's strategy with maximum ownership and results. Instead of the traditional separation of strategy design and implementation, *Strategy-In-Action* lets all stakeholders live and learn dynamically from the action. This book is hands-on, entertaining and efficient—and sure to add value to your company. Just do it!"
—DR. ALEXANDER V. HERZOG, CFO Ruf Group, CEO AVATECH & Ruf Services

"Most leaders and managers are drowning in information and the time clock of change continues to accelerate. Traditional strategic planning does not meet this rapidly evolving environment and new business paradigm. *Strategy-In-Action—Marrying Planning, People and Performance* provides a pragmatic approach and tool kit for strategic planning in our fast, globalized and wired world. Thomas and Ed have produced a practical template and checklists that can be used to guide, develop and sustain winning strategies. Most importantly, they combine the 'hard' elements of strategy planning with the 'soft' human elements that makes the difference in successful and sustainable execution. This is especially important given the dynamic social and cultural changes in business and the need for a more values-based, collaborative and empowering methodology. The book contains numerous interesting and practical case studies from their many years of business and consulting experience that emphasize a new logical, efficient and common-sense approach. A must read for anyone involved with strategic planning in the 21st century."
—DR. MARTIN CROSS, Chairman, Medicines Australia

"You laid the groundwork for our future. You were standing in our success as though it were your own. It is safe to say that without your input we would not be facing what we all now see is an extraordinarily bright future."
—CHARLES GRUMMISCH, Principal, Ascension Financial Strategies

"*Strategy-In-Action* is highly readable and filled with great examples. The title shows that strategy is not static or a one-shot exercise, but a dynamic and ongoing process. The building blocks are well-structured—you could use *Strategy-In-Action* as a checklist. 'Boiling It Down' sections at each chapter ending provide orientation and help readers find their way into the chapter later. I especially appreciated the focus on leadership styles and culture during the strategy process, since culture eats strategy for breakfast any day."
—Markus Hotz, Chairman, Insights Schweiz AG

"This is the rare business book that goes beyond theory and actually helps you accomplish. We made an outstanding return on our investment. When we started, we were fragmented all over the world. Now there is more transparency and inter-plant sharing of best practices; people contribute beyond their perimeter. We uncovered the value of our people and leaders; now we will keep empowering the teams. We no longer hide issues but put them on the table; we are much more imaginative, finding new ways to meet the goal. I can only say: Read *Strategy-In-Action*, apply its methods to your enterprise, and you will get a very good payback and personal satisfaction."
—ALEXANDRE FIGUEIREDO, Vice President, Comfort & Trim Systems, Faurecia

"I especially appreciate your perspective to imagine we are already at our goals and identify what the organization looks like in the future as a framework for establishing strategy now."
—KURT A. FLOSKY, Executive Vice President, FAAC Inc.

"Having experienced various team building exercises over the years that did not fulfill my expectations, I was quite skeptical at the start about this methodology. I have changed my mind. We have used Strategy-In-Action to create a shared understanding of what was missing or blocking us, we aligned on a joint vision and strategic intent, and we carried out 28 catalytic projects aimed at causing breakthroughs that we can now scale up or replicate (or, if one failed, take it off the agenda). I recommend this book to any senior manager who needs to mobilize a large-scale, complex organization for the future."
—BRUNO LE STRADIC, then Director Earth Observation, Navigation & Science Satellites, Astrium, an EADS Company

"A crucial book and approach that will change the way you see—and do—strategy. In the 21th century, leaders have to cope with day-to-day operational constraints and at the same time stand in a strategic future. Being this kind of stategist is a huge challenge. Thanks to the *Strategy-In-Action* approach and tools we offer our clients, for several years now, a new way of thinking, communicating, acting and getting results. Congratulations, Thomas and Ed, you awake people to be the change for the future of their companies."
—JEAN-GUY PERRAUD, President, Hexalto

"This is the only strategy book I know that gives a truly holistic view of strategy. It integrates strategy alignment, highly pragmatic execution and performance, and the human element in one seamless process. Call it my professional bias, but I especially liked the people component, which is all too often lost in the strategy literature—and more importantly in the process."
—DR. FRANK WALTMANN, Head of Learning, Novartis AG

STRATEGY-IN-ACTION

Marrying Planning, People and Performance

Dr. Thomas D. Zweifel and Edward J. Borey

Contents

Preface

If you are going through hell,
keep going.
—Winston Churchill

At a workshop a few years ago, a strategic planning expert said that strategy is like building a bathroom: you hire the plumber, choose the design, put in the plumbing, buy the toilet bowl and the appliances, install them, paint the bathroom, and so forth. Most workshop participants nodded in agreement and took keen notes.

Four months later, the mortgage crisis hit that ended up taking down venerable companies like Lehman Brothers, and pushed other venerable companies, like AIG, to the edge of the abyss.

We argue that these two events are connected. The mainstream way of thinking about strategy not only gives "experts" a bad name. It is also the type of thinking that fails in practice. And it is possibly the type of thinking that contributes to companies getting stuck in the status quo.

Already a decade before, we had asked ourselves what strategy approach would yield sustainable success. Now that the crisis rocked the United States and reverberated around the world, causing millions of people to lose their jobs, their homes, and their investments, it dawned upon us that the calamity was merely a symptom of a deeper malady. Corporate and government strategy is all too often designed behind closed doors and imposed top-down, the implementers have no voice in its design, and most stakeholders are either cogs in the firm's wheel or excluded from strategic thinking altogether. It is no wonder that this linear, one time, A-to-B approach is inadequate to meet the demands of an increasingly dynamic environment that imposes a higher velocity of change with each passing day. Traditional strategy is good for building a house or a sewage system for Mumbai, it simply is not good enough for unpredictable change, or for any endeavor that involves people.

It dawned upon us that business must retool its strategy principles and practices, or it will be condemned to repeat history and be rocked again by the tsunamis that get unleashed when planners devise static, top-down strategies for nations or companies, as happened from Chrysler to GM, from Circuit City to The Sharper Image, from Linens 'n Things to Germany's Escada, from Air America Radio to Wachovia, from Bear Stearns to Washington Mutual, from Lehman Brothers to Iceland's Landsbanki.

Makes sense, you might say, but why yet another book on strategy? After all strategic planning, its do's and don'ts, successful and failed strategies have been the subjects of many books, articles, and seminars. And much material out there is really useful. To give a highly partial and subjective tip of the iceberg: Michael Porter's comprehensive works on market analyzing, market strategies and long-term competitive advantage are a must for anyone in the business of creating and executing strategies. Porter's *Competitive Strategy* was about understanding markets, a company's competitive position in them, and strategies in response. His *Competitive Advantage* dealt with building value chains for lasting competitive advantage. In *Crossing the Chasm, Inside the Tornado, Living on the Fault Line*, and *The Gorilla Game*, Geoffrey Moore looked at strategies and tactics for building shareholder value in emerging companies and markets. Although targeted at high-tech Silicon Valley startups, Moore's concepts proved relevant for all firms in fast-paced markets.

Sumantra Goshal and Christopher Bartlett, in *The Individualized Corporation*, showed the importance of involving stakeholders in strategy design. The late C.K. Prahalad highlighted *The Core Competence of the Corporation*, and later the near-limitless reservoir of resource-poor entrepreneurs for innovation, *The Fortune at the Bottom of the Pyramid*. Prahalad collaborated with Yves Doz on learning from best practices worldwide in *The Multinational Mission: Balancing Local Demands and Global Vision.*

In extensive interviews for *Built to Last* and *Good to Great,* Jim Collins and his team explored common characteristics of successful companies. Larry Bossidy and Ram Charan's *Execution* focused, as the title said, on getting things done. They discussed key components of developing a corporate environment that meets commitments effectively.

But how do you do it?

There is a dearth of books about the real, down-to-earth *How* of managing strategy design-and-implementation in the 21st century, with its multiple stakeholders, empowered consumers, culture change, the Internet, transformative technologies, and constantly changing strategic landscapes. When the rubber meets the road, how do you build vision and strategy in a way that your people align around them? How do you get the perspectives of all key stakeholders without watering down the focus or wasting time? How do integrate the strong egos of your executives in the team without losing creativity, ideas or innovation? How do you combine planning and action in a single seamless process? How do you mobilize people for strategic, catalytic action? How do you deal with pushback, with breakdowns in communication, with domestic implementers or international partners who feel left out? How do you make sure you get early feedback from the action so you can see if you're on the right track before it's too late—and before you run up millions of dollars in sunk costs?

"What we are really trying to do," said David Ulrich, a professor of business administration at the University of Michigan, "is say that leaders need an integrated set of tools around both behaviors and results which will deliver firm strategy and the combination of behaviors and results." That is exactly right—in theory. As Albert Einstein put it tongue-in-cheek, "In theory, theory and practice are the same. In practice, they are not." Exhortations to "engage all parts of the organization" or "invite people" or "maximize participation"[1] or the principle that "Strategy making must be subversive" or "democratic"[2] are completely correct but woefully inadequate. They sound good on paper, but so what? How does that help you on Monday morning in the office when push comes to shove and things go so fast that you cannot see the wood for the new trees that have grown over the weekend?

With all due respect, few strategy gurus or consultants ever had to run sizable companies and test their noble and well-meaning prescriptions in the action of producing results. We have. Ed Borey spent his early career in a series of positions with Global 1,000 companies and later as COO, CEO, chairman, and board member in small- and mid-cap public company environments. Ed is a veteran of strategy design and execution. Before joining the board of Arotech (where he ran into Thomas), Ed had seen a lot. He led multiple turnaround initiatives, grew one company from $300 million to $800+ million revenue, led another through a Chapter 11 restructuring, brought two public companies private, and has acquired, consolidated or divested multiple operations.

As CEO of Swiss Consulting Group from 1997 through 2012, named a "Fast Company" by *Fast Company* magazine in 1998, Thomas D. Zweifel has worked with 40+ Fortune 500 companies as well as government and UN agencies, entrepreneurs and the military, on strategy alignment and execution, coaching one team to produce $74 million in additional revenue and another to achieve $200 million in cost savings. Not least, he again and again had to swallow his own medicine and test his strategy approach on his own company to this day (he was CEO of Swiss Consulting Group from 1997 through 2012). We have both worked with CEOs *and* implementers on the frontlines enough to know what it takes to build alignment company-wide, turn large ships around, facilitate large-scale change, and mobilize people for decisive action that matches the organization's strategy.

Ed and Thomas met in November 2006, at a Board of Directors strategy session of a high-tech company. We were both struck by how one of us would delve into an idea and the other would build on it. Without even talking to each other before the meeting, one of them would play bad cop with the company's chairman when the other was diplomatic, and vice versa. On the first break, when Ed went to De La Concha Cigars on Avenue of the Americas, Thomas spontaneously joined him. On the way back Thomas said he had been working on a book about strategy and asked Ed if he might like to co-author the book. Ed agreed on the spot. The result is what you are holding in your hands. You be the judge whether or not it was a good strategic move; at the risk of being biased, we think so. Marrying Ed's four-decade track-record as a CEO, Board Member, General Manager and all around troubleshooter with Thomas' three decades of building strategy alignment and developing leaders on the job, in the action of producing breakthrough results, brings about innovation to both strategy and leadership.

We call it "Strategy-In-Action"—a holistic approach to the formulation and execution of strategy. It is about designing strategy not based on theory or lofty principles, but in the aftermath of action. It is about converging strategic and day-to-day operational activities into one seamless boost that drives the organization forward. It is about the dynamic human factors involved in developing and executing a strategy, and the methods for best results.

Overview

This is not theoretical. We have perfected the process over time, in the action and through much trial and error. The framework reaches from analysis to design, execution, to after-action review of results and back to analysis again. *Strategy-In-Action* aims to give CEOs, board members, and senior managers seven simple—though not always easy—building blocks. Written from the vantage of the CEO, it is applicable to all those within the company who need to overhaul company strategy and/or build a shared and actionable strategy, and for all those in government, nonprofits or the military who need innovative strategies to carry out the people's business and/or make change.

Strategy-In-Action stands on three core principles. One, strategy and execution must be twins joined at the hip. Strategy without execution means at best opportunities lost and resources wasted, and at worst forgotten files that gather dust on the shelves of oblivion. Execution without strategy means blind activity that leads to poor results and unintended consequences. Two, each phase of the process is equally important. And three, who "the strategists" are is transformed. The participation, alignment, and commitment of the company's most important resource, its people (stakeholders, gatekeepers, decision-makers, implementers, even end-users) is critical to making it all happen.

The book flows organically so managers can use it like a cookbook. It is full of cases and stories that illustrate what works and what does not; and these stories are from all sectors, corporate and government, non-profit and military. We go with Peter Drucker who said that all organizations are essentially the same in that they all have to organize people to meet organizational goals, whether they are a business or a government agency, a church or an army.

Chapter 1 explores why traditional strategy is bankrupt and sifts through stories and cases in search of the answer. It gives a mini-history that leads up to the predicaments we now face, shows how the world has changed and how strategic planning has failed to catch up, since conventional strategic planning suffers from eight fallacies. Chapter 2 asks what is different about Strategy-In-Action and comes up with thirteen differentiators. Each of the next seven chapters focuses on one of the seven steps of Strategy-In-Action. Chapter 3 shows how to forge a shared understanding, the foundation of broad-based alignment across company levels, functions and regions. Chapter 4 is about building a joint strategic vision that inspires all stakeholders, gives focus, and serves as a magnet for action. One of its stories is how even the automotive industry, which has been rather stuck, is experiencing a jolt of energy from some visionaries.

In Chapter 5 the reader learns how to co-create the "dashboard" (as Jack Welch liked to call it when he was at GE) of key performance indicators, and how to avoid counter-productive metrics. Chapter 6 is a guideline for generating the drivers—thrusts and synergies—based on all the analysis and design work so far. Chapter 7 covers three key elements that must be integrated in strategy but are all too often overlooked or avoided: Leadership, power, and culture. Chapter 8 is about the component of Strategy-In-Action that ties together design and implementation: catalytic pilots that test the strategic assumptions in the laboratory of action and yield quick wins.

The final step, in Chapter 9, is essential to the cyclical nature of Strategy-In-Action as a process not a project: how to sustain momentum by getting feedback from the action to the strategy, standardizing strategy and action, and scaling up. The book concludes with Chapter 10, a troubleshooting guide designed to help leaders in the action when push comes to shove. The chapter provides one of the most potent techniques that separate leaders from the pack: how to not be stopped by a breakdown, but instead use breakdowns as raw material for breakthroughs.

Acknowledgments

We thank our clients, our companies and our colleagues who have helped us develop and test our approach in the laboratory of the market for three decades (and in Ed's case, four) and led us to a highly predictable strategy approach for addressing the increased challenges posed in the 21st century. We thank our previous readers for their interest in and feedback to our ideas.

Thomas' wide-ranging conversations with Tapas K. Sen fifteen years ago led to an article and stimulated the original idea for a book on Strategy-In-Action. Thomas is also grateful to Harry Korine for helpful suggestions and challenges to our ideas, Stefan Hangartner for a helpful review of the manuscript, and Dov Gordon for throwing himself into the game head-first without really knowing how. Thomas is indebted to The Hunger Project for pioneering the planning-in-action methodology, and for freely sharing its intellectual property.

Ed is grateful to Homer Hoard, Mike Anderson and Mark Parrish as CEOs who took an early interest in him, worked with him to evolve his strategic skills, and gave him his first strategic playing field. He also thanks long-time Organizational Development and Strategic practitioners Patricia Moore and Ron Scott for years of discussion and collaboration in developing the Strategy-In-Action framework.

Above all, we are grateful to our families. Susan Borey has been best friend, wife, closest advisor and partner to Ed for four decades. Gabrielle, Tina and Hannah give Thomas a future to live for, without which strategy would be meaningless.

CHAPTER ONE

Is Strategy Dead?

In theory, theory and practice are the same.
In practice, they are not.
—Albert Einstein

Norbert Reithofer, CEO of BMW, recommended that his board members read *The Black Swan*. The book has shown that seemingly impossible events—black swans—tend to happen, and that they have especially strong effects, as did the breakdown of Lehman Brothers that plunged the world economy into a crisis, precisely because nobody expects them. At a time of extremes, Reithofer says, predictions have become impossible.

Gone too are the times of certainty for Reithofer's countryman Wolfgang Reitzle, chief of Linde, a 1.5 billion euro company that makes gases for the energy, chemical and food industries. "It has never been more difficult than today," Mr. Reitzle said, "to give a precise prediction of future economic development."[3]

When seemingly plausible scenarios smacked up against reality in the most recent recession, it dawned upon executives "that strategic planning doesn't always work," in the words of the *Wall Street Journal*. That's putting it mildly. "This downturn has changed the way we will think about our business for many years to come," said Office Depot chairman and chief executive Steve Odland in an interview. Walt Shill, head of Accenture's North American management consulting practice, was more blunt: "Strategy, as we know it, is dead."[4]

Is that so? Or is strategy evolving to a model that is more of a match for this century? What we know: traditional planning does not allow

1

for the flexibility, adaptation, or accelerated decision-making needed in times of rapid and unpredictable change. This insight is far from new; it has been a growing realization for CEOs and strategists for the past two decades with the advent of the Internet and e-commerce, a globalizing economy and virtual teams, flattening corporate hierarchies and free agents who are much less loyal to the company than the "company men" of one or two generations ago.

Some companies have weathered sea changes in global markets and become dynamic catalysts, including Amazon, Apple, Caterpillar, Google, IBM, Intel, Microsoft, Nordstrom, Novartis, Nucor, Procter & Gamble, Starbucks or 3M, to name a few. But they are exceptions, and they cannot rest on their laurels. Others have had difficulty recognizing innovations, shifts in the marketplace or even understanding their marketplace's needs in the first place. Nokia, swallowed by Microsoft in late 2013, is only the latest example. A generation ago, Swiss watch companies were in for a rude awakening. They had been the main producers of wristwatches at least since 1790, when the city of Geneva alone exported over 60,000 watches a year. By the mid-18th century Swiss watchmakers had exported some 500,000 watches. By the turn of the 20th century they ruled the global watch industry; by 1968 they commanded over 65 percent of the watch market worldwide and over 80 percent of industry profits.

Throughout their undisputed reign, they had held on to tried and true rules of the game, doggedly producing the same first-class watches with high-quality and expensive manual labor. But by 1970 their luck turned; nimble Japanese copycats dumping their low-cost, high-quality watches on world markets outmaneuvered them. Unlike their skeptical Swiss competitors, leading Japanese watchmakers like Hattori-Seiko embraced the new quartz technology eagerly and benefitted from a massive drop in costs: The average production price of a quartz watch plummeted from $200 in 1972 to 50 *cents* in 1984. ₅The result: By 1989 Seiko alone produced some 15 percent of the 690 million watches worldwide, while Switzerland's watch industry took a nose dive, and 50,000 of 62,000 Swiss watchmakers lost their jobs. In 1970 there had been 1,620 watch companies in Switzerland; fifteen years later their number had shrunk to 600, and their world market share was down to a meager 15 percent.

Ironically, the researchers who had developed the first electronic quartz watch were, of all people, Swiss. But when they introduced their cutting-edge idea at a 1967 conference of Swiss manufacturers, it was roundly rejected. Yes, the quartz watch performed like a watch, it looked like a watch, but it lacked "real watch" components like gears and mainsprings. In short, it did not fit the Swiss watch paradigm.

If the Swiss watchmakers suffered from too much attachment to the past, the Swiss bank UBS suffered from too much derring-do, at least until August 2007, when Peter Kurer, the bank's then-general counsel, thought he deserved a vacation. A tumultuous summer had seen the forced closing of an in-house hedge fund and the ejection of the bank's chief executive. Enough was enough. But when Kurer returned from a lazy sailing turn in Corsica, things got only worse. By the middle of 2007, UBS had amassed more than $20 billion in super-senior collateralized debt obligation (CDO) tranches. Reportedly, and amazingly, senior investment banking executives had no idea these tranches existed: "We had twenty people on the beach looking at grains of sand when the tsunami came and wiped everybody out," said one banker familiar with UBS operations.[6] The tsunami did roll in and the tide turned. In October 2007, the bank revealed its first losses of $4.4 billion, and several high-ranking executives had to stand down. In December, as UBS prepared to announce a further $10 billion loss, Mr. Kurer and other executives hurriedly arranged for a much-needed cash injection from the Government Investment Corporation of Singapore. Another $4 billion loss followed in January 2008. How could UBS, which had made a name for itself as one of the most prudent global banks, take one of the biggest blows of the credit crisis? To be fair, UBS was not alone: A bubble of loose credit had made some companies reckless. In the United States alone, 152 financial institutions went bankrupt, filed for bankruptcy protection, or closed down and went into receivership during the crisis. How come nobody saw the tsunami coming? What had gone wrong?

Financial services companies were not the only ones to suffer. Take the U.S. automobile industry. For 77 years in a row, in good times and in bad, General Motors sold more cars than any other company. But in the first quarter of 2008 another company beat GM's sales by 160,000 more cars: Toyota. The Japanese multinational even embarked on a joint venture with GM designed, in part, to help the venerable firm revamp its production system. But despite over 3,000 articles analyzing its best practices, and although its principles were widely copied, Toyota continuously stayed ahead of the pack[7]—at least until its 2010 recalls for unexplained braking problems hampered its reputation, and its chairman Akio Toyoda was forced to admit to the U.S. Congress that "Quite frankly, I fear the pace at which we have grown may have been too quick."[8] But even amid its woes, the world's biggest carmaker saw U.S. sales surge 41 percent in March 2010 from a year earlier (and in China and Japan 33 percent and 51 percent respectively), while several of its U.S. rivals flirted with bankruptcy. For too long, U.S. carmakers had focused on North American demand for large cars and trucks when fuel costs were low, and ignored the increasing marginal cost of union labor content in each vehicle produced. Why couldn't GM or Chrysler prevent their fall from grace at the time (their fortunes have improved since then)?

Or take media and entertainment: how can traditional media deal with new media, especially the onslaught of targeted online advertising? Will "old" media like newspapers, magazines, or television soon be out of business? The ailing recording industry, despite hunting down illegal downloads of its songs and albums, saw sales of CDs plummeting by 15 percent, to 500.5 million units, from 2006 to 2007 alone. During the same period, music sales online rose by 45 percent to 844.2 million tracks; by April 2008 Apple Inc.'s iTunes Music Store had become the top U.S. music retailer.[9] By 2010, iTunes sold 70 percent of all music downloads worldwide, making it the world's largest legal music retailer—seven years after its inception. The trend is clear: music has moved to the

Internet. How can traditional record companies, book publishers, and print media deal with the shift?

In games, Nintendo, Sony and Microsoft's Xbox are under siege from Angry Birds, Fruit Ninja and other inexpensive, or free, downloadable games, particularly for mobile phones and tablets. After shipping close to 100 million Wiis, in 2012 Nintendo did something unimaginable just a few years ago: it posted its first-ever loss in its era as a video games company. Nolan K. Bushnell, founder of Atari and godfather of the games business, said that game consoles may soon be too expensive for few but the hard-core players: "These things will continue to sputter along, but I really don't think they'll be of major import ever again." The company has made strong comebacks before, but it faces a big obstacle: Nintendo's games play on its own devices only. Should it change its strategy and create games for devices made by other companies, including the hundreds of millions of iPod Touches, smartphones and tablets out there? "It's the hardest strategic decision Nintendo has had to face in a long time," said Robbie Bach, the former head of Microsoft's Xbox business.[10]

In education, massive open online courses, or MOOCs, harness the power of crowd-sourcing technology to offer elite college-level courses—once available to only a select few, on campus, at great cost—for free, to anyone with an Internet connection.[11] The first MOOC of note was in 2011 when Sebastian Thrun, a Stanford University professor, offered a free artificial-intelligence class—attracting 160,000 students in 190 nations. A wildfire ensued; other elite research universities like Harvard, Princeton and MIT, as well as online course companies like Udacity, Professor Thrun's spinoff; edX, a joint venture of MIT and Harvard; and Coursera, a Stanford spinoff, have sprung up to offer open higher education to everyone. The price tag: zero. This development presents challenging questions: How can lower-tier universities compete and convince their students that their courses are worth the price of admission? What about quality assurance of the product—how can plagiarism be prevented? What will the millions of students now enrolled in hundreds of online courses actually learn? And what should be the business model that will allow universities and education companies to make money with MOOCs?

In transportation, the global airline industry broke back into the black in 2007. The airlines had made great strides in streamlining. They had improved their fuel efficiency by 19 percent since 2000 while cutting non-fuel costs by 18 percent, and achieved a net profit of $5.6 billion, for the first time in seven years. But they had little time to celebrate. Several companies flew into nasty weather when in April 2008, ATA, Aloha Airlines, and Skybus suspended operations and filed for bankruptcy. One major carrier, Delta, said its fuel costs would rise to $2 billion that year alone. "Oil skyrocketing above $130 per barrel has brought us into uncharted territory," said Giovanni Bisignoni, director general of the International Air Transport Association. "Add in the weakening global economy and this is yet another perfect storm."[12] Globally the industry lost $50 billion in the past decade—$11 billion in 2009 alone.[13] To cover their ballooning costs, many airlines raised fares, added fuel surcharges, and charged travelers $25 or more for checking a second bag. (Some airlines now make passengers pay for their first bag too.) Not to mention the declining on-board service. Business travelers are all too familiar with the policy on most domestic U.S. or European flights that they must pay for sandwiches; American Airlines charges for wine on flights to and from Europe.) Dean Headley, co-author of the Airline Quality Survey, said of the industry: "Oil prices have forced them to say, 'We can't consider the customer as much as we'd really like because we have to stay in business.'"[14] The price hikes could not have come at a worse time. Facing a slowing economy themselves, many business and leisure travelers had to cut back on their flying. Ulrich Schulte-Strathaus, secretary general of the Association of European Airlines, said that the "business model" of the industry "is changing out of all recognition."[15] Why hasn't the airline industry—with a few valiant exceptions such as Southwest—come up with actionable strategies?

In energy, British Petroleum suffered a major blow to its reputation in the spring and summer of 2010 when the "Deepwater Horizon" oil spill in front of the Louisiana Gulf Coast produced the largest man-made disaster in United States history. But the root cause, despite what many analysts claimed, was not faulty equipment or bad drills or bad crisis management. The real problem lay with the company's top-down decision-making, its exclusion of key stakeholders from strategy design and even from day-to-day operational decision-making. By June 2010, BP's go-it-alone attitude and shortsighted strategy had taken a heavy toll: its stock had lost more than $100 billion, or more than half its value.

Governments are just as affected as business by short-term thinking. Back in the 1960s, the National Aeronautics and Space Administration (NASA) spent $24 billion (in 1969 dollars) to send twelve astronauts to the moon, $2 billion per astronaut. But in the generation after the Apollo program ended, the engineers who carried crucial knowledge in their heads either retired or died, or both, without ever passing their know-how on to their colleagues. Important blueprints were either catalogued incorrectly or not at all, and the people who drew them up were no longer around to draw them again. The result: NASA is now reinventing the wheel. The estimated cost to American taxpayers (in 2005 dollars): $100 billion.[16] How could that happen?

And NASA is but one agency. What should be the strategy of the United States (or any country for that matter) in the twenty-first century? For example, how can the United States fight global terrorists not organized in hierarchies but in loosely connected cells—in one word, networks? Military planners talk about NetWar, which requires strategies utterly different from the good old days of nation-against-nation warfare or the equally frightening but quite neat and orderly bipolar world of the Cold War.

Finally, bad strategy affects international organizations. The World Bank rolled out a $300 million plan to supply rural African farmers with hand-pumps to improve safe water. The noble initiative suffered from one problem: The pumps were designed with men in mind. Planners in Washington, D.C. had fallen prey to a common misperception—not surprisingly, since when we hear "African farmer," most of us picture a man;

but 80 percent of Africa's food is grown by women farmers (the only sector where men produce more than women do is in housing and construction). So the World Bank delivered pumps too large for women; only men could use them. Worse, the Bank failed to train locals in repairing the pumps, since illiterate farmers could not read the instructions; they simply threw the pumps away when they broke and returned to their age-old practice of using contaminated public cisterns or murky ponds. The result was untold disease, from typhus to malaria, not to speak of $300 million down the drain.

A Micro-History of Strategy

Not surprisingly, strategy approaches reflect the times in which they are conceived. That is not to say there are no lessons to be learned from history. And much of the work done has been of great value. As the Spanish philosopher George Santayana wisely said, "Those who do not remember the past are doomed to repeat it." In this context, we propose a mini tour of strategy history. The idea is to get at the key historical underpinnings of the current strategy paradigm. We want to find the nuggets that can help us build the strategic approaches of the future. Below is a sampling of some of the major ideas that have influenced our thinking.

Sun Tzu (6th century BCE), a contemporary of Confucius, was a Chinese general who lived in the state of Wu and worked as a mercenary, the equivalent of a modern military consultant, for king Helü of Wu. Sun Tzu proved his leadership competence by training a battalion of untrained females, whose leaders were none other than close concubines of the king himself. Sun Tzu's efforts enabled Helü to conquer the state of Chu and turn Wu into the most powerful state of the period. Then Sun Tzu disappeared, and the exact date and place of his death are shrouded in mystery. His treatise is usually translated in Western editions as *The Art of War,* and though both Stalin and Mao are said to have

8

read the work while they made their wars, Sun Tzu did not advocate warfare but rather a set of philosophies for avoiding conflict and still retaining control in a tight situation with an adversary. "All warfare is based on deception," he wrote.

> Hence, when able to attack, we must seem unable; when using our forces, we must seem inactive; when we are near, we must make the enemy believe we are far away; when far away, we must make him believe we are near. Hold out baits to entice the enemy. Feign disorder, and crush him.[17]

Chanakya (350-283 BCE) was an economist (the world's first one, some say), a professor at Taxila University, and later the prime minister of the Maurya Empire in ancient India. He is traditionally credited as the author of *Arthashastra*, a treatise on statecraft, economic policy, and military strategy (*artha* is Sanskrit for worldly, wealth; *shastra* means science). Called by some the "Indian Machiavelli," he counseled a king to take calculating and sometimes brutal measures to preserve his realm and the common good, for example by using spies to keep his eyes open for strategic intelligence. But Chanakya also taught how to be a wise and virtuous king—for example, how to set up a legal framework and run an efficient government bureaucracy. He even devised a daily schedule for the ruler to run the affairs of the state in 90-minute increments (for example, "First 1½ hours after sunrise: Receive reports on defense, revenue, expenditure; First 1½ hours after sunset: interview with secret agents").

Niccoló Machiavelli (1469-1527) was, of course, the Italian renaissance political philosopher who came to be elected second chancellor of the Republic of Florence. Like Chanakya, Machiavelli counseled a prince, in the book *Il Principe*, how to rule his state. He got his ideas from observing the soldier and churchman Cesare Borgia, who built his reign in central Italy through a strategy of self-reliance and prudence, force and intimidation and, at times, cruelty. Much like the Indian strategist almost two millenia before him, Machiavelli was a realist, less concerned with how things should or could be than with how they actually were. In an ideal world, Machiavelli would have liked *virtú* (virtue), but he had to make do with the less-than-perfect world he faced.

> I have thought it proper to represent things as they are in real truth, rather than as they are imagined. Many have dreamed up republics and principalities which have never in truth been known to exist; the gulf between how one should live and how one does live is so wide that a man who neglects what is actually done for what should be done learns the way to self-destruction rather than self-preservation. The fact is that a man who wants to act virtuously in every way necessarily comes to grief among so many who are not virtuous.[18]

Karl von Clausewitz (1780-1831) was a Prussian senior army officer, military historian and influential military theorist famous for his dictum that "war is merely a continuation of politics with other means" and for his—and the West's—principal treatise on the philosophy of war, *Vom Kriege* [*On War*], still studied at military academies today. Before Clausewitz, armies were led by a country's king or ruler himself, which made that country vulnerable to extinction, much like in chess: Lose the king and you lose everything. Armies the world over owe Clausewitz, and a group of enterprising young officers around King Frederick the Great, the idea of the general staff, an important innovation after the defeat of the Prussian army by Napoleon. The idea was to spread authority across a cadre of officers selected on a competitive basis, not on their family lineage. Officers could be trained and exchanged, making the army more like a machine and less vulnerable to defeat. Instead of a single commander at the helm now stood an anonymous "General Headquarters" or G.H.Q. of an elite officer corps, a term still in use by most of today's corporations.

Max Weber (1864-1920) was the sociologist (although he saw himself as an economist and historian) who conceived of the modern bureaucratic organization with rules and regulations, duties, distribution of authority, and clear competencies needed to function effectively. To Weber, one key feature of all large-scale organizations was "the unchanged and continued existence, if not [for] the establishment, of pure bureaucratic administrations." Such an administration usually became a well-oiled apparatus: "The fully developed bureaucratic mechanism compares with other organizations exactly as does the machine with the non-mechanical modes of production." This machine exists "without regard for persons." It is strictly hierarchical, just like Clausewitz's military structure: "The bureaucratic structure goes hand in hand with the concentration of the material means of management in the hands of the master." Weber already saw one pitfall of bureaucratic organizations: "Once it is fully established, bureaucracy is among those social structures which are the hardest to destroy."[19] Bureaucrats would do almost anything to preserve the status quo and the machine itself.

Frederick Taylor (1856-1915), a contemporary of Weber, was the father of what came to be called "scientific management." He believed that the industrial management of his day was amateurish, that management could be an academic discipline, and that by analyzing work, he would find the "One Best Way" to manage. He streamlined operations, cut costs, eked out the last ounce of productivity from workers, and treated the organization like a machine, minimizing input and maximizing output. In 1893, Taylor opened an independent consulting practice in Philadelphia; his business card read "Systematizing Shop Management and Manufacturing Costs a Specialty." In 1898, Taylor joined Bethlehem Steel, which would serve as his principal case study. For his process of treating high speed tool steels he received a personal gold medal at the Paris exposition in 1900, and was awarded the Elliot Cresson gold medal that same year. In his famous time and motion study, Taylor broke a job into its component parts and measured each to the hundredth of a minute. One of his studies involved shovels. He noticed that workers used the same shovel for all materials, calculated that the most effective load was 21½ pounds, and found or designed shovels that for each material would scoop up exactly that amount. Taylor was forced to leave Bethlehem Steel in 1901 after feuds with other managers, and was generally unsuccessful in getting his concepts applied; it was largely through the efforts of his disciples that industry came to implement Taylor's ideas. (Nevertheless, the book he wrote after parting company with Bethlehem Steel, *Shop Management*, sold well.) Taylor's approach had a terrible side effect: it compounded a type of thinking that has robbed the production process of the quirky stuff that produces innovation and gives people satisfaction. Taylor himself wrote that "our scheme does not ask for initiative in a man. We do not care for his initiative... We do not ask our men to think."[20]

Alfred P. Sloan (1875-1966) is widely seen as the father of the modern industrial organization. Since 1899 he had been president of Hyatt Roller Bearing, a maker of roller and ball bearings. Once Hyatt merged with United Motors Corporation, which eventually joined General Motors, Sloan rose to Vice-President, then President, and finally Chairman of the Board of GM. Under Sloan the carmaker became famous for managing diverse operations with financial statistics such as return on investment. Sloan established a pricing structure in which Chevrolet, Pontiac, Oldsmobile, Buick and Cadillac (from lowest to highest priced) each belonged to distinct price segments so they would not compete with each other. Customers could be kept in the GM "family" as their buying power and preferences changed while they aged. These concepts, along with Ford's resistance to this innovation in the 1920s, propelled GM to industry sales leadership by the early 1930s. It held the pole position for over 70 years. Under Sloan's direction, GM became the largest, most successful, and most profitable industrial enterprise the world had ever known. A Sloan Foundation grant established the MIT School of Industrial Management in 1952, charged with educating the "ideal manager," and the school was renamed as Alfred P. Sloan School of Management, still now one of the world's top business schools.

These approaches, from Sun Tzu to Sloan, have helped shape the foundations of twentieth-century management and strategy. They were largely mechanistic, treating organizations like Swiss clocks, with people as cogs that could be moved around at will. They assumed a strict hierarchy and thought that the princes or planners at the top had all the necessary intelligence (as Churchill put it, "The higher you rise, the more you can see the big picture of vision and strategy"). They lived in a simpler world of a few powerful nation-states where the enemy lines were clear and markets were mostly local. Above all, they lived in a world where time moved slowly and in a linear fashion, and where the future was pretty much an extension of the past.

The New Landscape: Seven Facets

But the world has changed in at least seven ways that have completely upended traditional strategy approaches and have rendered the old rules of the game obsolete.

Speed. A few years ago Seth Brady, a 747 cargo pilot, was mystified when a former employer dispatched a Learjet out of Toledo to meet a British Airways flight at JFK because GM had come up five seat backs short at its Chevrolet Corvette plant. "They flew in the extra Corinthian leather from England, put it on the Lear at JFK, ran it up to Pontiac, made the new seat backs in three hours, put them back on the Lear, and took them to Bowling Green, Kentucky, in time for the production line not to shut down." The pilot wondered especially "how anyone could afford to fly all these airplanes around"—until he was told that hauling the cargo by air was cheaper than the cost of shutting down the assembly line, which was $42,000 per *minute*.[21]

The dizzying pace of advances in technology, demands from customers, and attacks from competitors who didn't even exist a few days ago (or so it seems) has cut down the time between action and reaction. It has become commonplace to say that an "internet year" is three months. The number of text messages sent and received each day exceeds the total population of the globe. Also daily, more than 3,000 new books are published. According to BBC News a new blog is created *every second*, and the number of blogs doubles, on average, every five months.[22] Our children will use technologies, consume products, and face issues that don't even exist today. The sheer speed at which information turns up, gets transacted, and is compressed into new knowledge disrupts traditional strategy.

Globalization. In the first quarter of 2008 IBM, based in Armonk, NY, earned 65 percent of its revenue outside the United States. Mumbai-based Tata, India's tech-services giant, collected 51 percent of its revenue in North America.[23] The five percent of China's population—or, if you prefer, the seven percent of India's—with the highest IQs are now more numerous than the United Kingdom's entire population. The full implications of the globalizing economy for strategy are difficult to grasp and are described in detail elsewhere[24], but this much we know: The global market has changed the game.

Internet and Virtual Organizations. The Internet has created a revolution of distributed personal empowerment. If Facebook were a country, it would be the third-largest country, would house one in seven of the world's inhabitants, and would likely be the largest country in Earth by 2016. People search Google 2.7 billion times each month. Nine out of ten teenagers (at least in industrialized countries) now have a home computer, mobile phone, and games console—but 72 percent of teachers never play computer games.

The workforce is in transition. Knowledge workers switch jobs and even careers several times during their productive lifespan. One out of two people now works at a company he or she has been with for less than five years. More and more people work in virtual teams, either because of outsourcing activities to back offices in Asia, Latin America or Africa, or because of telecommuting. Most workers still travel to their workplace, but telework is on the rise: a 2007 survey found that 23 percent of American workers regularly do their job from someplace outside the office, and 62 percent of respondents who cannot work off-site would like to.[25]

New Technologies. Technologies are constantly changing. PayPal allows people to do banking without banks, Skype to call people without a phone, iPhones to buy train tickets without money. And this is only the beginning; already 3D-printers are commercially available that print pretty much anything you want, from in-soles for your daughter's shoes to a spare part for your drill to a cover for the Tupperware box you lost, based on a design you simply download from the Internet. Possibly within the next generation, nanotechnology (technology the size of some millionths of a meter) will allow people to assemble products molecule by molecule. This could fundamentally transform the economic process of production and consumption, as consumers would be able to have small manufacturing plants and make their own products right at home on their kitchen counters.[26]

Democratization. When Sloan and Taylor were around, there were only a handful of democracies in the world. Top-down organization was the norm. Today, organizations are flattening, automating repetitive functions or cutting out middle management to cut costs and stay competitive. For companies, democratization means user-generated innovation: Users are now participating in designing products from windsurfing equipment to Google applications to mountain bikes.[27] They make their own videos and upload them to YouTube, the world's second-largest search engine after Google, its parent company. They post their music on YouTube. They self-publish books. At the same time, managers find themselves in the fishbowl of scrutiny by share-holders and the media. There is more public accountability than ever before, and more demands for profitability and compliance. Growing cynicism about public and private organizations, their intentions and their effectiveness makes for a daunting challenge of doing the right thing and doing it right.

Empowerment. The way Taylor, Sloan, and their contemporaries used people was simply a reflection of their times. The human being was an object, a commodity, human capital at best. People did not ask questions. If they did, they would ask, "What *should* I do?" Thomas' father worked for 35 years at Sandoz, which later became Novartis; he would come home many an evening and express his frustration at the company—but he never seriously questioned the need to work there. The next generation (at least in the West) changed all that. After the late 1960s they started asking: "What do I *want*?"[28]

Complexity. The business of doing business has become more complex. Some estimate that a week's worth of information in *The New York Times* is more than the average human in the 18th century was likely to come across during his or her lifetime. The English language now has about 540,000 words—five times the number when William Shakespeare was alive. The business problem is to make sense out of all of this—to turn information into knowledge. But no one person, or even one board of directors, no matter how brilliant or experienced they are, can see the whole picture anymore. The new world is far too complex for anyone to master alone.

Combined, these facets produce changes that are virtually impossible to foresee, let alone plan for. (That is probably why in 2008 McKinsey opened a "Center for Managing Uncertainty" to capitalize on a recession-rattled environment.) The very idea of strategy has come under attack. The management thinker Henry Mintzberg and his collaborators were not the first to criticize the process of strategic planning; already in the late 1990s, a burgeoning literature on hyper-competition suggested that formal strategic thinking is doomed to failure given an ever-changing business environment.[29] Not to speak of technological innovations such as search, e-commerce, PayPal or social networks.

Undeterred, Porter declared in an interview with *Fortune* in 1999: "The arrival of the Internet will affect every industry in some way, but for 50% or more of the economy it's not a transformational event. It will have a powerful impact on the supply of information to customers and the relationship between companies and their suppliers, but it's not like the automobile. You don't have to change the theory of strategy to deal with the Internet."

Porter may be right about the Internet in isolation; the Web might not transform strategy theory in and of itself. But combine it with the other forces that drive the 21st-century economy, from globalization to outsourcing or off-shoring, from democratization to flattening hierarchies, from knowledge workers to free agents, and you find that the *practice* of strategy must change if companies and other organizations are going to survive, and thrive, in an ever-changing environment. Perhaps the massive changes in the last generation haven't changed strategy itself. But they create both an opportunity and a demand for changes in how you go about designing and implementing strategy successfully. And that changes everything.

The Eight Fallacies of Planning

When strategy fails, the question comes up, was it bad strategy or bad execution? Take Dell, which changed the game in the personal computer business by cutting out the middleman and selling directly to consumers. The "Dell Model" was once synonymous with efficiency, outsourcing, and tight inventories, and was taught at Harvard and other top-notch business schools as the epitome of smart strategy and outthinking the competition. But for the last seven years, the company has been plagued by serious problems, including misreading the desires of its customers, poor customer service, suspect product quality, and improper accounting. Is Dell's decline a function of a mistaken strategy or mistakes in implementation? It is probably a little of both. "Dell, as a company, was the model everyone focused on ten years ago," said David B. Yoffie, a professor of international business administration at Harvard. "But when you combine missing a variety of shifts in the industry with management turmoil, it's hard not to have the shine come off your reputation."[30] Traditional planning approaches tend to ignore the trends and the new landscape above, and fall prey to unrecognized and unexamined biases, blind-spots that filter out critical information and thereby stifle the creativity and productivity that lie hidden within organizations. We have seen eight fallacies that can become roadblocks to successful strategy.

The Reification Fallacy: "Strategy is a thing." Planners (and many of their colleagues) tend to see strategy as a blueprint, a plan, a book, a product that is finished and stable once it is done, and all you have to do is roll it out. This may work if you are building a bridge or the canalization system for Mumbai; but it fails as soon as human beings enter the equation. Today strategy can't be viewed as fixed, instead it has to be a dynamic and self correcting process. We use the word process to denote an ongoing paradigm as opposed to a project or program with discrete start and stop points.

The Control Fallacy: "I'm in charge—whatever I say will trickle down and be implemented." Some years ago, Ed interviewed a technology executive about his approach to planning, decision-making and execution. He found out that the executive's approach was to gather all the data he could, go off and think about a solution, declare that solution and have his people execute. While this approach gives him control, it discounts the value of his direct reports and does not grow executive talent around him.

18

Harvard Professor Clark Gilbert deplores the fact that "some of our colleagues who have studied strategy (and some consultants who advise on strategy) ... assume that once you design strategy it gets executed. They don't look inside the process."[31] Overconfident planners may think that the strategic process can be unilaterally controlled from the top. In today's highly complex environment, control is an illusion. Even if it were feasible, control would still be counterproductive because it tends to shut off local leadership, initiative and innovation by front-line people. After 9/11, even the U.S. Army's top brass realized that the soldier on the ground in Sadr City or Seoul has strategic intelligence that the Pentagon planners need.

The control fallacy has a mirror image: Middle managers are loath to question their bosses openly, like in the story of the Korean Airlines co-pilot who never doubted the pilot's judgment when the pilot made a stupid decision. "He is the pilot," the co-pilot later testified, "so I thought he must know what he's doing." The result: the plane crashed.

The Linearity Fallacy: "Strategy can be broken down into mini-tasks and performed predictably." Traditional planners believe that strategy is a step-by-step, linear process. It is not. Random House once bought a one million square feet warehouse for its vast catalogue of book titles. The problem was that a new technology, print-on-demand, made vast inventories redundant. The New York City-based publisher was stuck with a huge empty building and huge sunk costs. All too often, top managers don't change strategy when conditions change on the ground. This leads to unintended consequences instead of predetermined results.

The Path-Dependency Fallacy is a close cousin of the linearity fallacy. Since it is much harder to change an organizational structure or culture once it has taken hold, the future tends to depend on the past. Many planners (and managers) think incrementally. They are paid for minimizing risk—on the theory that you must avoid mistakes at all costs, or the sunk costs will be huge. Whether because of their personal risk-aversion, their fear for their job, or their lack of authority, they are unlikely to cast a bold and unpredictable vision. If things go well, they are complacent, meaning stuck in the past; if things go badly, they keep doing the things that worked last time. The consequences of such path-dependency can be bad for strategy execution, as Professor Gilbert pointed out in an interview.

> For example, senior management at a U.S. newspaper company says, "We need to get into the Internet, we need to prioritize this and make a big investment." But then at the operating level of the firm you have a sales rep who is used to selling a display ad for $40,000. The new business has a lower gross margin, the customer who is buying it isn't the rep's traditional customer, and the price point isn't the same. And so that sale rep says, "Well, I can sell a $40,000 display ad, or I can go out and find one of these new customers and sell them a $2,000 banner ad." Every day as that sales rep comes into work he makes a resource allocation decision at the operating level—how to allocate his time and attention—which de facto keeps the investment from happening, even though financial resources have been procured.[32]

The "People – Things" Fallacy: "People are expendable or exchangeable." One Fortune 500 company went to the extreme; to save money, it planned to offshore some 5,000 IT workers, which made people skittish, sank company morale, and sent the most resourceful people (the most valuable players) running for other employers (usually a competitor). The sunk costs were significant, because unlike technology, human ingenuity cannot be copied or reproduced.

The Hard/Soft Fallacy: "Strategy is a hard skill; people issues are soft." Many planners think that only "hard" issues like strategy, finance, and operations really count, and that "soft" issues like communication, culture or relationships are luxuries, an afterthought, nice to have but not essential. Others shy away from the "soft" stuff because people issues are inherently unpredictable, messy, and hard to manage systematically. Yet people issues are just as often the primary source of good or bad results.

The Fortress Fallacy: "Management's job is to run the business, not to get distracted by what is happening outside." Some planners fail to understand the forces of the environment and their impact on the organization. Or they talk—and listen—only to people who share their interests or their biases. But success and failure are driven largely by the entrepreneurial ecology around the organization (or country, as we see in the next fallacy).

The Ethnocentric Fallacy: "Our business is mostly domestic." CEOs and their strategic planners tend to think that their strategy is a national matter. But national borders are increasingly meaningless in the face of global flows of goods, services, capital, people, and information. An exclusively national mindset can make planners blind to understanding outside influences on their domestic market dynamics (recall the Swiss watch industry's doldrums above).

In the words of Robert Evans, the brash and flamboyant former Hollywood producer famous for his memoir *The Kid Stays in the Picture*: "Never plan, kid," the old-time movie tough said, because "planning's for the poor."[33] Evans was not exactly an expert, but in a sense he was right: In today's Internet Years and highly volatile markets, old-style strategic planning is inadequate to meet the task. So what can be done? What strategy approach can avoid these fallacies? The good news, despite this chapter's title, is that strategy is far from dead, it is just fighting the last generation's war and struggling to make the evolutionary leap to be relevant in today's environment.

$\sim$

Boiling It Down

❑ There has never been a greater need for good strategy and execution than today. And the overwhelming majority of organizations pride themselves of having a strategy. So why does strategy fail so often? Why did industries as diverse as Swiss watches, U.S. car manufacturers, education, media, or airlines fail to prepare for what was coming?

❑ The current strategy model has a long history that ranges from Sun Tzu to Machiavelli to Clausewitz, all the way to Alfred Sloan and Frederick Taylor in the early twentieth century. Their principles have shaped for hundreds of years the paradigm of how strategy has been practiced.

❑ But the world has changed. Speed, globalization, the Internet and virtual teams, new technologies, democratization and flatter hierarchies, empowerment and the growing importance of the knowledge worker, and increasing complexity have combined to change fundamentally how companies must do business. In a complex, dynamic, and uncertain world, traditional planning methods are non-starters.

❑ Traditional approaches tend to suffer from eight fallacies: linearity, path-dependency, control, reification, people = things, hard/soft, fortress, and ethnocentrism. A new approach is needed.

CHAPTER TWO

Long Live Strategy (-In-Action)!

All men can see the tactics whereby I conquer,
but what none can see is the strategy
out of which great victory is evolved.
—Sun Tzu

Most people take the Internet so for granted—except perhaps when they can't get online at a Starbucks or an airport—that they have forgotten the original impetus for this path-breaking medium, or the process that brought it about. But if we look at the story of the Internet carefully, we might see the building blocks that allow us to rethink what strategy can be. As you read the story below, look for the underpinnings of the strategy approach that gave birth to perhaps *the* breakthrough innovation of the 20th century.

Case: The Birth of the Internet

In 1948, right after World War II and in the midst of Cold War theorizing about nuclear warfare, the U.S. government set up the Advanced Research Projects Agency. ARPA soon became the cradle of connectivity that, more than half a century later, was to spawn the era of Google and YouTube, Twitter and Facebook, Amazon and WebMD. It was then that a bunch of engineers with slim ties, hackers with long hair, and other visionaries built the foundations for a world-changing technology.[34]

A decade later the Soviet Union launched Sputnik and shocked the American government and public out of business-as-usual. "Sputnik in 1957 surprised a lot of people," said Bob Taylor, who left NASA to become the third director of ARPA's computer science division, "and Eisenhower asked the Defense Department to set up a special agency so that we would not get caught with our pants down again." The heat was on, and ARPA created an environment in which breakthrough innovation could happen. "ARPA was a go-for-broke kind of culture," Taylor recalled. "First of all, ARPA had a lot of carte blanche. If ARPA asked some cooperation from the air force or the navy, they got it instantly and automatically. There was no interagency bickering. It had a lot of clout and little or no red tape. To get something going was very easy."

Then, in 1960, Paul Baran, an electrical engineer working at the Rand Corporation, invented one of the Internet's building blocks. "We didn't have a survivable communications system," he recalled, "and so Soviet missiles aimed at U.S. missiles would take out the entire telephone-communications system." The U.S. air command had only two forms of communication at the time: the U.S. telephone system and shortwave radio. The danger of a Soviet attack seemed likely: "the collateral damage was sufficient to knock out a telephone system that was highly centralized. Well, then, let's not make it centralized." The answer was packet switching. Rather than sending data alone one path, as a traditional telephone circuit does, packet switching breaks data into chunks, or "packets," and lets each packet take its own path to a destination, where the packets are reassembled. Packet switches became the crucial hardware for sending and receiving bursts of data in a decentralized network.

By 1966, Bob Taylor was connected to several time-sharing systems at various universities and think-tanks, which was a pretty clunky and cumbersome affair, since "for me to use any of these systems, I would have to move from one terminal to the other. So the obvious idea came to me: Wait a minute. Why not just have one terminal, and it connects to anything you want to be connected to? And, hence, the Arpanet was born." The clincher came when Taylor went to raise money for his discovery. "I went over to Charlie Herzfeld's office and told him about it. And he pretty much instantly made a budget change within his agency and took a million dollars away from one of his other offices and gave it to me to get started. It took about twenty minutes." In funding a venture like the Arpanet, the government showed what fellow engineer Steward Brand called "pretty enlightened leadership."

Some private-sector companies did not show quite the same entrepreneurial spirit, to say the least. Take the venerable American Telephone and Telegraph. "Working with AT&T would be like working with Cro-Magnon man," Taylor recalled. "I asked them if they wanted to be early members so they could learn technology as we went along. They said no. I said, Well, why not? And they said, Because packet switching won't work. They were adamant. As a result, AT&T missed out on the whole early networking experience."

In 1969, ARPA gave the job of building interface message processors (IMPs, another name for packet switches) to another private firm, Bolt, Beranek & Newman. (The late Senator Edward M. Kennedy gave several people at the company a good chuckle when he sent a congratulatory telegram in which he referred to IMPs as "interfaith" message processes.) Larry Roberts, the engineer who issued the bid, says: "There were two competing bids that were particularly close, BBN and Raytheon. And I chose between them based on the team structure and the people. I just felt that the BBN team was less structured. There wouldn't be as many middle managers and so on."

The historic moment came on September 2, 1969, when the first IMP was connected to the first host at UCLA. It was the beginning of the Internet as we know it. But the event was hardly historic. "I mean, who noticed?" asked Leonard Kleinrock. "Nobody did. Nineteen sixty-nine was quite a year. Man on the moon. Woodstock. Mets won the World Series. Charles Manson starts killing these people here in Los Angeles. And the Internet was born. Well, the first four everybody knew about. Nobody knew about the Internet." As late as the early 1990s, when Marc Andreessen, then a student at the University of Illinois, created Mosaic, the first browser to take off, the Internet still seemed like the best-kept secret. "When we were working on Mosaic during Christmas break between 1992 and 1993," Andreessen recalled, "I went out at like four in the morning to a 7-Eleven to get something to eat, and there was the first issue of *Wired* on the shelf. I bought it. In it there's all this science-fiction stuff. The Internet's not mentioned. Even in *Wired*."

Bob Metcalfe was then a bearded MIT grad student. For some reason the hyper-geek was entrusted with the job of demonstrating the Arpanet system at a conference in 1972 at the Washington Hilton. "And as I'm giving my demo, the damned thing crashed. And I turned around to look at these ten, twelve AT&T suits, and they were all laughing. And it was at that moment that AT&T became my *bête noire*, because I realized in that moment that these sons of bitches were rooting against me. To this day, I still cringe at the mention of AT&T. That's why my cell phone is a T-Mobile. The rest of my family uses AT&T, but I refuse." Metcalfe was to have the last laugh, though: He went on to invent Ethernet and to found 3Com. And he came up with Metcalfe's Law: as the number of users on a network grows, the value of that network grows exponentially. This became the underlying principle without which networking sites such as Facebook, dating sites like Match.com, or markets like eBay or Craigslist would be unthinkable.

Steve Case, who in the 1990s had built AOL on these network effects, recalled: "The biggest breakthrough that drove the success of the medium was getting P.C. manufacturers to bundle modems into their P.C.s. We tried for several years with all of them, but finally convinced IBM to do that in 1989. Up until then modems were viewed as a peripheral." It was one of the first commercial breakthroughs in the new medium, and it was to change everything: "In just a short few years we went from a business nobody knew anything about or cared about to suddenly being such a part of everyday life that the system was down for a day and it was a major national story. It was like the water system was down or the electricity system was down."

It was a true transformation. How that happened makes for a perfect story of how strategy works at its best. It's decentralized, since nobody can know everything. You can't see very far into the future, but you have a vision and push for that vision with decisive action every day. It's dynamic, not static. Progress is not linear, but comes in evolutionary leaps. And these leaps are not brought about in the boardroom, but in the action—action taken by many leaders, indeed many nameless leaders, who have a vision, the freedom to experiment and play, and "the freedom to fail while daring greatly," as Teddy Roosevelt once put it. One of the leaders who rode the commercial wave of the Internet, Barry Diller, said it best when he looked back on his success in turning QVC, his home-shopping television channel, into an interactive Web enterprise: "It was one dumb step in front of the other. I wasn't interested in travel. What happened is, I said, Oh my God. What a great idea to colonize travel by the Internet. What a great idea. And so we did it, and it turned out rather well. There were no road maps or signposts. You were making it up every day."[35]

Rebooting Strategy

Making it up every day. If that is true for strategy now, then what *is* strategy now? The story goes that a young strategy consultant was asked how he would define "strategic." After looking dumbfounded for a moment, he said he couldn't define it, he simply knew a strategy when he saw one. Let's take a fresh look, and start by saying what strategy is *not.* In the late 1990s the strategy guru Michael Porter weighed in on the debate: "there's a lot of confusion out there about exactly what strategy is," he said, "and a lot of dangerous practice."[36] Porter drew a useful distinction between *operational effectiveness* (including concepts like time-based competition, Total Quality Management, lean manufacturing or reengineering) on one hand and *strategic positioning* on the other. "Operational effectiveness means you're running the same race faster," Porter said. "But strategy is choosing to run a different race because it's the one you've set yourself up to win." His work stressed that a company needed to build strategy in the context of external forces and opportunities shaping its industry. He defined strategy as building sustainable long-term competitive advantage.

Some strategy experts challenged Porter's work. Instead of his outside-in model (from external factors—rivals and new entrants, substitutes, suppliers and buyers—to strategy), Gary Hamel and the late C.K. Prahalad focused on an inside-out model (starting with the core strengths of the organization and building its strategy on them). Joseph Bower and Clark Gilbert found that companies might have an intended strategy, but the strategy that actually emerges can be quite different. They defined strategy as "the actual aggregation of commitments and their relationship to the realized strategy of the firm,"[37] and explored what internal or external factors might lead to the gulf between intention and reality.

Our way of defining strategy is etymological, going back to the roots of the word. It stems from the Greek *strategos*, a mix of *stratos* (army) and *ago* (leading) that makes for "the leader or commander of an army, a general." So at its source, the meaning of strategy brings leadership (back) into the game. And despite the fact that Greek democracy featured a lottery system in which people were periodically selected for government or other leadership positions, much like in the U.S. jury system today, leadership is now much broader than in ancient Greece. Democratization and flatter hierarchies, the diffusion of knowledge through the media and the Internet have produced a "flat world," as *New York Times* columnist Thomas Friedman put it. Above all, the importance and role of the human element has changed. As we saw in Chapter 1, the number of people who now have the chance to don the mantle of leadership is far larger today than a generation ago. Even those who are not in traditional senior leadership roles may have access to strategic intelligence; people like the receptionist or the frontline salesman communicate with customers every day and are often closer to the market than top managers or directors in boardrooms. So by saying that strategy must include leadership, we mean something very different today than it meant a generation ago: the strategy process must be based more broadly than ever. Secondly, in our view strategy is simply a bridge between vision and action/results/winning. Strategy is a moving target, it must constantly change in response to the new landscape given by the action, and it must be systematically and regularly challenged to stay relevant. Hence it must be more dynamic now. Rather than a business plan or a book or a document, a good strategy provides openings for action—in other words, irresistible opportunities for decisive moves—and a freedom to be—in other words, it unfetters people's leadership, creativity, and innovation. It must treat people not as an afterthought but as the key agents and co-creators of strategy. Above all, it must be consistent with the axiom that "strategy happens in the action, not in the office."[38]

29

The Strategy-In-Action Difference

All too often strategic planning did not meet such exacting standards. It reflected the prevailing centralized hierarchies. It was a lengthy, and more often than not tedious, the process emanating from the C-suite and driven through the ranks on a top-down basis in a succession of educational meetings, coordination sessions, and pep talks. Agreement—or more accurately, compliance—was achieved through pre-specified formats designed to execute strategies pre-cooked at the top. An elaborate and pre-ordained system of meetings and presentations resulted in molding the goals and actions into the company's strategic plan, which was usually accumulated in one or several financial presentations. The books often went on the shelf or into a filing cabinet, the task was checked off, and usually the plan did not see the light of day until years later when the next planning cycle came around.

Ironically but not surprisingly, the solution came not from business but from the field of international development. In the 1980s, David Korten, a Stanford-trained expert on transforming bureaucracies into responsive systems that could serve human development, wrote that "development would need to become not simply people-*oriented*. It would need to become truly people-*centered*..." In Korten's model, all stakeholders are strategists, since "everyone from shop worker to company president becomes a contributor to a continuing process of strategic adaptation. Strategy development becomes a total organizational process" where not only board members and managers, but also frontline people, and ultimately even key suppliers, customers, and lobbyists, have a voice. But if strategy becomes everyone's concern, what is left for the bosses to do? A lot, Korten wrote: senior managers

> act to build diversity in their strategic "gene pool," by nurturing
> centers of creative deviance within their boundaries. The result is a

reserve of alternative strategic capacities which may be called upon as needed. The dominant values are service and a belief in the creative potential of people.

While the stakeholders must be strongly aligned on a common mission, they need not agree. In fact creative dissent and even deviance from established wisdom and group-think are needed for innovation and the constant renewal of the organization.

This was a powerful call to action, but Korten's was a lone voice in the wilderness. Few heard his call, least of all in the business community, and virtually no companies applied his insights. Combining Korten's model with the seminal works of the late C.K. Prahalad and Gary Hamel, namely their "Strategic Intent" article and our own insights into strategy and capacity-building over 25 years, we have found in our work with Fortune 500 companies, small and medium enterprises, and startups that what we call Strategy-In-Action is eminently applicable to business and yields consistent results. Table 2.1 (on the next page) sums up the essential differentiators between traditional planning and the Strategy-In-Action process. In a nutshell, Strategy-In-Action is the marriage of strategy formulation and execution in a process that thrives on change and unintended consequences; feeds them back into the process; and reformulates strategic objectives based on the action.

A disclaimer is in order here. Strategy-In-Action does not mean "adhocracy," a governing style former President Bill Clinton's administration became famous for. Clinton aide Richard Haass borrowed the term from Roger Porter, who had coined it in the 1980s when he had served as the elder George Bush's domestic affairs adviser. Haass granted that "Adhocracy is not all bad.

It enables a new President—especially one with little experience in the Washington shark tank—to learn about people. It also speeds the emergence of new ideas and policies... And adhocracy is less prone to leaks... Best of all, adhocracy is flexible. Task forces are ideal for special situations and crises when full-time focus is called for.

Haass's chief examples are John F. Kennedy, who created the Executive Committee, a group of wise men who steered the United States through the Cuban Missile Crisis, and Franklin D. Roosevelt—one of the more ad hoc U.S. presidents—who got the country out of the Depression and through World War II. But he readily concedes that "the drawbacks of adhocracy far outweigh the benefits." Adhocracy might discourage debate and dissent. Meetings—the real ones, where sensitive information is discussed and decisions are made—include only the in-group, so people might not say the truth for fear of being left out. Nobody is fully accountable for a policy or decision. Often there is confusion about the policy itself. Adhocracy is error-prone and can suck up the leader's time. Worst of all, Haass wrote presciently—in 1994—that adhocracy's emphasis on personal relationships leads individuals to think too much about protecting the boss.[39]

Traditional planning	Strategy-In-Action
Stable, static, linear	Dynamic, nonlinear, mission-driven
Incremental; expand what the organization does well	Entrepreneurial leaps; identify the next strategic breakthrough and transform the organization to achieve it
Track record determines the future	Track record is one baseline variable in projecting future results

Strategic and functional fit; produces within current capacity	Strategic tension between now and the future; ambitions are out of proportion to current resources and capabilities
Strategy "for"	Strategy "with"
People as recipients	People as co-authors and key agents
Focus on structure and process	Focus on results and winning
Minimize change or risks	Call forth change, encourage manageable risks
Organizational silos	Integrative, systemic
Outside experts	Knowledge lies in the team, self-reliance
Problem-solving	Future-based

Table 2.1: Traditional Planning vs. Strategy-In-Action

Strategy-In-Action is not a euphemism for improvisation. It is a deliberate and systematic process, not an excuse for crisis management or making it up as you go. It is made of seven building blocks (see Figure 2.1 below): Shared understanding; Strategic intent; Strategic thrusts or objectives; Indicators of success; Leadership; Catalytic actions; and Sustaining momentum. Chapters 3 to 9 each illustrate one phase with stories and tools for how to (and how not to) do it. Here is a quick overview.

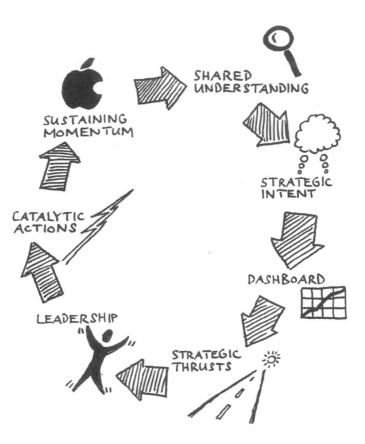

Figure 2.1: The Strategy-In-Action Cycle

Step One: Shared Understanding. Key stakeholders from all segments of the company come together to face the facts and forge a shared understanding of the current situation. The group combines top, middle and front-line managers, and at times other stakeholders such as board members, suppliers, investors, and perhaps even customers or regulators.

Step Two: Strategic Intent. Long-term vision serves as a stabilizer in times of uncertainty. Strategic vision is a statement of what is possible to achieve, is worth achieving, and represents a new quality of life for all stakeholders. The strategic intent is a magnet that pulls the present to the future, big enough to provide vision, yet short-term enough for each participant to wrap their arms around it and be energized.

Step Three: Dashboard of Indicators. Key performance indicators measure the achievement of the strategic intent. These metrics on the "dashboard" must be consistent with the strategic intent and measure the future, not the past; they must be designed to pull for desired actions; and all members of the organization must own them and commit to them.

Step Four: Strategic Thrusts. Thrusts are not merely milestones along a linear path to a goal but a set of objectives needed to achieve the strategic intent. Each is a major building block that provides what is missing for achieving the strategic intent, removes key blockages, seizes key opportunities, and closes the gap between the current reality and the strategic vision. Each thrust stands on its own, yet works synergistically with the others.

Step Five: Leadership. Leaders can be at all levels of the organization. There are four types: those who lead the strategic process itself, typically Board members and C-level executives; implementers; other affected stakeholders; and gatekeepers who might throw a wrench into the process unless they are aligned. They are capable of leading by example; unyielding about the goal but flexible about the means; highly curious and tolerant of uncertainty; and respectful of divergent viewpoints.

Step Six: Catalytic Actions. Catalytic actions are pressure cookers that alter the landscape of what is possible, which in turn informs and transforms the strategy by providing rapid feedback to the strategy. Catalytic projects are designed to be short term, low-cost and low-risk, so as to learn from the action without betting the farm. They can be *ground-breaking* projects that explore innovative new ways of achieving objectives, and *proof-of-principle* projects that demonstrate with sufficient authority that successful innovations can be scaled up or serve as a basis for strategic decisions.

Step Seven: Sustaining Momentum. The final phase is about creating a sustainable learning organization. Participants take stock, communicate successes, learn from innovations elsewhere, engage others, and enrich the strategy for the next round of the process. The aim is institutionalizing successes while getting rid of non-starters. Here you converge strategy with day-to-day operations in seamless continuous improvement.

More about that in subsequent chapters. For now, we underline that Strategy-In-Action is not an event. It does not happen once, and you cannot check it off like just another item on your checklist. Rather, it becomes the framework, the context in which *everything* happens. Strategy-In-Action is an attitude, a way of being and thinking that you integrate in your day-to-day. "We want people to use these techniques daily in their work—using broad insights; learning faster; failing faster," says Cindy Tripp, marketing director at Procter & Gamble Global Design, about the process (P&G calls it design thinking). It is rather a new way of thinking for the $80+ billion global consumer products giant. Managers who have been with the company for many years describe P&G's former attitude: Design used to be seen as "the last decoration station on the way to market."[40] That has changed fundamentally, and now that the process is embedded in P&G's culture, it can never go back to the old ways. But how do you do it? Let's go to the next chapter to get the ball rolling. The first step is to get your (and by "your" we mean everybody's) hands around what's at hand now.

~

36

Boiling It Down

❑ A strategy model that works for the 21st century must be more than people-oriented; it must be people-*centered*. It needs leaders with a bold vision, leaders who are unencumbered by bureaucratic rules, leaders who have the freedom to fail while daring greatly, as Teddy Roosevelt once put it.

❑ The history of the Internet provides us with such a model. Who created the World Wide Web? Visionary leaders who had champions behind them backing them up; who married strategy and action; who scoffed at hierarchy and protocol; and who had the guts to take risks and entrepreneurial leaps.

❑ Strategy-In-Action combines strategy design and execution into one systematic, unified, and inclusive process, a dynamic continuum of strategy—action—strategy—action—strategy... The feedback from results to strategy improves not only the execution but the strategy itself.

❑ The seven phases of Strategy-in-Action process are: Shared understanding; Strategic intent; Strategic thrusts; Indicators of success; Leadership; Catalytic actions; and Sustaining momentum. Strategy exists in a continuum with action.

CHAPTER THREE

Face the Facts: A Shared Understanding

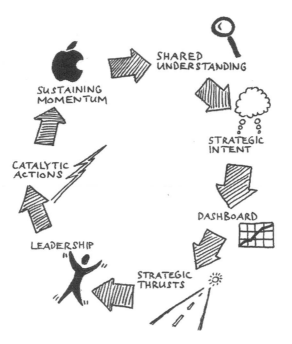

...three-fourths of the things
on which action in war is based
lie hidden in the fog of uncertainty.
—Carl von Clausewitz

When Jill Barad became chairman and CEO of the toy company Mattel in January 1997, the company's stock was worth $27.75. In fourteen months, under her leadership, it reached a high of $45.625. In November 1999 it plunged to $13.375, half of the value when she had taken the helm. What had happened? To her credit, Barad had turned Mattel's flagship Barbie from $250 million into a $1.7 billion brand.

But her greatest asset became her gravest liability because of her over-reliance on that one star product and her inclination to self-delusions. She had a bad nose in financial analysis, overvaluing and overpaying acquisitions. She was great at marketing but poor at operations.

Those shortcomings might have been redressed, by the specialists she hired, were it not for another weakness: Barad's unwillingness to listen to people, for example customers, retailers or employees, who disagreed with her. She lost more than a dozen top managers in the two years after taking the company's reins. One former senior Mattel executive said: "When I've seen her at ad and marketing strategy meetings, everything she says improves the quality or the strategy. But as a long-term strategist and as a developer of people? No. An ability to accept an alternative point of view? No." Few executives dared contradict Barad; customers who complained to Mattel were ignored.

"A lot of it was an obsession with the bottom line, and they were riding on their high horse and not listening to their customers," one retailer said. "Not listening to the dealers and the customers is now a major part of their problem."[41] Ignoring or bulldozing alternative views robbed Barad of vital intelligence. At the same time, Barbie had become Barad's winning formula, resulting in a lack of innovation in other areas at Mattel. "Jill is one of the most brilliant, hard-driving marketing product people I have ever met," said a top executive at a major toy retailer. "Her problem is, the world is not just Barbie. Not everything in the toy business can be done the same as Barbie."

Mattel paid dearly for Barad's failure to get an unvarnished view of reality: In the first quarter of 1999, the company lost $171 million—despite a 7 percent surge of Barbie sales worldwide—and its third-quarter profits fell by 55 percent. The company's stock had fallen almost by half.[42] Barad lost her job (although her severance package of some $50 million sweetened the blow).

If anyone close to the company claimed to be shocked by the news, they would have deluded themselves. The writing had been on the wall, and a more perceptive board might have seen the early-warning signals. As early as 1995, when Barad was still chief operating officer, company insiders expressed concerns about her leadership. In a June 1995 speech to senior managers, James A. Eskridge, then the newly installed president of the company, ran through a short list of challenges facing Mattel, including what he called simply the "Jill Factor," a cryptic reference to Barad's erratic management style. One danger, Eskridge added, was the company's tendency to operate according to what he called the ostrich school of reality. Eskridge left the company shortly after Barad was named chief executive[43] so his dissenting voice fell under the table.

More than a decade later Mattel kept smarting from a lack of shared understanding. In the last quarter of 2008, its sales fell 11 percent, or $2 billion. So in 2009 the company came up with a new idea: taking aim at hundreds of millions of potential adult customers—especially young, urban professional women—in China. Mattel opened a six-story Barbie flagship store in Shanghai selling, along with the iconic dolls, luxury items such as gourmet chocolate, animal-print scarves, and $10,000 wedding dresses designed by Vera Wang. The gambit seemed to be working; the store was mobbed by young women who saw Barbie as a symbol of the lifestyle they aspire to. But the jury is still out on whether this idea is pie-in-the-sky or based on a solid understanding of the Chinese market.

That is what this chapter is all about. A company's leaders must systematically cut through their own myths, face the facts, and build common knowledge of what is really going on in- and outside the firm. In other words, they must build a shared understanding that all key stakeholders can own. Note that unlike the sequence recommended by many strategy experts, Strategy-In-Action does *not* begin with articulating a vision because building a vision in a vacuum is like shooting in the dark. You must start with a diagnosis shared by the key stakeholders, or the vision will be built on divergent views of reality. This brings us to the first rule. (There are six.)

Rule 1: Involve Enough of the Right People

The Netherlands boasts the largest and most elaborate system of flood defenses worldwide, so one would think the Dutch government knows all facets of the issue, but it happens to the best. Here is what happened: when floods engulfed the Dutch coastal regions, the government decided that this should never happen again. In a billion-dollar investment, the ministry of transport went about a strategy to protect the coastline by building dykes. Halfway through the project, the environment ministry popped up and said, what about the environment? It turned out that the transport ministry had never consulted other stakeholders or considered external factors. The result was a wrong-headed decision; the sunk cost was huge.[44]

Why does involving the right stakeholders matter this much? Strategy formulation and execution are of course the responsibility of the CEO, with alignment and approval by the Board. Having said that, in our experience the CEO is best served by using a participatory process for several reasons. First, the complexity and velocity of the business environment makes broader participation a must so that issues can be seen from all sides of the business ecosystem. As we have seen, reality is often so complex that no single person sees the whole picture. A front-line person or a receptionist may have as much access to intelligence from the market—if not more—as top managers and board members, since they interact with customers and suppliers on a daily basis. If they and other stakeholders get to participate—hold the stake, as it were—in strategy formulation, they are simply more likely to implement the strategy.

As the late Stanford University head coach Bill Walsh put it: "Winning teams are more like open forums in which everyone participates in the decision-making process, players and coaches alike, until the decision is made. Others must know who is in command, but a head coach must behave democratically. Then, once a decision is made, the team must be motivated to go ahead and execute it."[45] Walsh, who took a downtrodden 49ers team and led it to Superbowl championship within three years, could have said the same about masterful strategists.

Second, as our colleagues Bob Johnston and Doug Bate put it succinctly in their book *The Power of Strategy Innovation*, "People support what they help create."[46] Look at your own life: did you ever implement something that you had no voice in designing? What would be your level of commitment to a strategy if nobody asked for your input, invited your buy-in, or gave you the chance to own it?

And third, democratization in the workforce and flattening hierarchies give people more voice and pull for participation; and common sense tells us that if two heads are better than one, with good facilitation 12 to 25 heads are usually better than one. Of course there is a healthy balance: On the one hand, involving nobody and imposing strategy unilaterally misses out on vital intelligence. On the other, involving too many people could slow things down or lead to leaks of vital company secrets. On one hand, how many people do you need to represent all points of view and explore all your options? On the other, what size group can manage the process effectively? Do you start with a small team and expand as the process develops, or go with a larger group from the start? We have found that working with at least twelve and at most twenty-five stakeholders strikes that balance. The exact number is of course company-specific.

The key stakeholders you cull for the strategy team will likely be very busy. Pulling them from their day-to-day pressures so they can focus on the broader picture of Strategy-In-Action can be an uphill battle. What compounds the challenge is that you cannot withdraw them from their operations for an extended time; that is precisely what makes them valuable to the process. And at least in the early stages strategy design adds to their standard duties.

Selection of the individual participants is not a casual decision. Since Stategy-In-Action exists in a continuous dynamic between strategy and action, you need to select the people that will not only formulate the strategy but will take action to realize it. Typically this includes your direct reports, mid-level management of critical areas, and individual contributors in very critical areas; or some combination of the three.

For a truly *shared* understanding that gets at the views of all stakeholders, the CEO or process sponsor gathers with the core strategic group to align on the major elements needed for the shared understanding. What matters is that they look broadly and systemically, and that the process be participatory. In 2006 we worked with a team of senior executives at a global bank in need of a comprehensive strategy for offshoring some 5,000 employees in its large IT department to places like North Carolina or India. The bank wanted cost savings while maintaining transparency and morale. We had to overcome resistance to ensure the project sponsor chose enough of the right people from every segment of the firm whose viewpoints might be relevant to a successful strategy: IT managers, executives from adjacent departments that interfaced with this department (either as clients or suppliers), such as private banking, investment banking, asset management, and technology infrastructure services, as well as corporate communications people; people at every level, from top executives all the way down to the developers who would be affected by the offshoring strategy. The temptation was strong to exclude people who might disagree with or dislike the project sponsor, or whose added value he did not recognize. In the end, getting these "difficult" people in the room paid off handsomely.

Rule 2: Tolerate Dissent

This brings us to the next ground rule: participants must listen and learn before jumping to conclusions. They must be open, honest and straightforward. They must communicate potently—if possible without blame, complaint, judgment or excuses.[47] They must postpone decisions until they have alignment. Above all, they must be willing to appreciate the views of other stakeholders, without expecting that same appreciation from others. They must trust that other participants might have a valid point of view too. The motto is, focus on understanding, not on being understood. That's what Carlos Ghosn did when Renault charged him in

1999 with bringing Nissan back from being close to bankruptcy. Before making hard decisions, he asked many different stakeholders in many different company segments and sought their input. "When I came to Nissan, I engaged in what I call 'active listening' with as many people as I could," Ghosn recalled in an interview. "I listened carefully, even to the opinions that totally contradicted my own beliefs, to make sure that when I made my decisions, I hadn't missed anything."[48] Despite enormous pressure to take action, Ghosn took care to listen to all points of view for what seemed a very long time to those who clamored for quick fixes. Ghosn promised that unless Nissan achieved its mission, he would be the first one to go. Ghosn's strategy paid off: He became the rare foreign-born CEO to achieve cult-like status in Japan. Mothers thought of him as the perfect son-in-law; he became a comic-book hero who would fly with his black cape into crisis-ridden corporations to save them. His willingness to listen and to lead by example had given him the badly needed consent and credibility—aside from vital market intelligence and input on the strategic intent—to make the tough changes that would ultimately return Nissan to market leadership (and vault Ghosn to the helm of Nissan's mother-ship Renault).

To illustrate how this works on the ground: on October 2, 1990—Mahatma Gandhi's birthday—The Hunger Project (THP), an international NGO on the roster of the UN, co-sponsored a meeting with India's planning commission to create a strategy for the end of hunger. The challenge was almost beyond words. At the time 11,000 people died each day from chronic hunger in India, one-third of the world's daily total. In an unprecedented move, THP assembled two dozen Indian leaders from all relevant sectors: government officials and business leaders, heads of nongovernmental organizations (NGOs), media people and experts. This was a coup. Over tea before the meeting started, several participants could be overheard saying to each other, "How could they get all these people into one room?" Some of them had worked for thirty or forty years in isolation. The government people in Delhi had made policy, thinking it would trickle down to the villages. NGOs had worked with the villagers, but without access to the big picture. Misunderstandings had been rife. So the first thing this collection of Indian leaders did was to express their profound frustration with each other. They did that for the entire first day of the conference.

Hunger Project officials were crestfallen. Was this meeting going to fail? Should they concede defeat, pack their bags and leave? What would be the consequences for their work in India as well as in all the other countries where hunger persisted?

Rule 3: Bring Back the Big Picture

In this moment of near-despair, Ramkrishna Bajaj rose to speak. He was one of India's most senior industrialists, head of the Bajaj group of industries and a member of THP's global board. His father, Jamnalal Bajaj, had been a financier of Gandhi's movement for India's independence, and Ramkrishna himself had served, in his own words, as "Gandhi's coolie" in his youth. Thomas still has a photo of Bajaj as a young man, standing with Gandhi at a train station and tabulating the money they had just raised.

Throughout the meeting, despite his stoic calm, Ramkrishna had grown increasingly restless. Now he raised his hand almost imperceptibly, in a typical self-effacing gesture, and rose slowly, as if he were tired. The room fell silent. Ramkrishna looked over all the participants through his large rectangular tortoise-shell glasses. Then he began: "My friends, it is quite sad for me that we are here, the best minds of India, all of us dedicated to the spirit of Gandhi-ji, and yet we are bickering and accusing each other of malice. Please, my friends, let us not forget our common mission— the mission that my father financed, the mission that Gandhi-ji always pursued, the mission to embetter the lives of the poorest."

Ramkrishna reminded the participants that people all over the world were watching them, were committed to them, and were waiting to hear about their strategy. "Do you know, my friends, that at this moment, while we are sitting here and debating each other, over six million people in 150 countries have joined the struggle? Do you know that close to a lakh (100,000, ed.) individual investors have invested their personal resources in our mission? Do you know that more than a dozen of them invest $100,000? These people are committed, and they are watching us."

In a few simple words, backed up by the enormous respect he commanded, Ramkrishna had painted a much bigger picture, a context vast enough to encompass all the opposing viewpoints in the room. There were many nods of agreement, and several voices called out, "Hear, hear." Suddenly the meeting began to work. Several speakers rose to acknowledge Ramkrishna's and his father's leadership. One could see that they were proud again to be Indian, proud of their independence, proud to be involved in fulfilling Gandhi's vision for India. The participants quickly aligned on the key points of a common understanding of the current situation. They recognized what was missing, what were the major blockages in the way of ending hunger, what were the opportunities not seized—and now they spoke without rancor, without blame, without complaint. Now they spoke the facts simply as they were. By the end of the day, delegates from various districts huddled together excitedly to draft action plans. Being confronted with the bigger picture had awakened them from their narrow viewpoints and stubborn righteousness. The realization had shocked the meeting into consensus.

Rule 4: Confront the Sacred Cows

In 1992, THP again worked with a government, this time Senegal, to hold a national planning meeting. Fitigu Tadesse, the organization's vice president for Africa, called from the global office in New York City to ask the government for a list of participants. He received the list, but without the women's names. Dr. Tadesse asked them politely to re-send the names. The Senegalese officials practically laughed him off: "Women? Why women? There are no women in this conference." The message was clear: Strategy is a male domain, and women are at best marginal to the task. It was not that Senegalese planners were bad people; they were simply caught in a blind spot and did not see the reality: that women cut the wheat, get water and firewood, clean the house, milk the goats, drive the buffalos into the lake, beat the laundry clean with a wooden bat, cook for the family, and carry the bricks to construction sites. "When we hear the words 'African farmer,' most of us have a picture in our minds of a man tilling the land," Holmes said. "But it would be much more appropriate to say, 'The African farmer and her husband.'"[49]

Case: Automakers and Blind Spots

To maximize creative thinking, you must be willing to challenge your own automatic assumptions and unwritten rules. When in late 2008 the recession hit, a deadly combination of high oil prices, the credit crisis and rising unemployment brought the U.S. auto industry to the precipice. Sales of the Big Three—General Motors, Ford, and Chrysler—collapsed to levels not seen since 1945. Credit dried up. Cash reserves dwindled. GM alone, once the world's mightiest industrial enterprise, was on the verge of bankruptcy. It hemorrhaged $1 billion a month, its stock was below its 1946 price, and it came dangerously close to being unable to pay its bills, with devastating results for the U.S. economy, since the Big Three employed some 250,000 people and about one of ten American jobs was in the auto industry. How could it come to this? Why did the Big Three fail so miserably while others succeeded?

One root cause was that they had not faced reality for a while. The Big Three (now called the "Detroit Three" since they were getting smaller) had been struggling for years as they lost market share to foreign competitors like Toyota, Honda or BMW that built factories in the United States and gained political clout. Take GM, which for years built uninspired, oversized cars that fewer and fewer people wanted. Saddled with lavish employee and retiree health benefits and rigid work rules that guaranteed inefficiency, the company paid its workers an average rate of $73 an hour, compared with $48 at Toyota's U.S. factories.[50] If the carmakers had faced the facts instead of marching on in the blind certainty that Detroit was too big to fail, they might have adapted to the realities of the 21st-century marketplace. But its managers did not wake up when Toyota entered the Nascar races in an attempt to out-American the Americans. And while the rest of the world developed smaller and more fuel-efficient cars, Detroit built mostly bigger SUVs and Hummers. Yes, the Detroit Three did come up with electric cars and hybrids, they promised super-frugal "supercars," yet in the end they kept producing only more giant cars.

Few top managers lost any sleep over this lack of realism. When the bosses of the three companies went to Washington D.C. for a bailout, they did not behave like people who wanted to make changes. They came separately, each in his private jet, as if they had not noticed that the game was now about saving energy and money. They came without a plan or answers to the urgent questions facing them. Their inability to kill their sacred cows nearly plunged Detroit into an abyss.

Unless you look carefully at the facts and separate them from your assumptions, your entire strategy will lead you in the wrong direction. Disentangling the facts from the myths is one of the foundation stones of the strategic process. The global financial crisis that started in 2007 is only the latest logical result of governments and too many companies rushing headlong into uncertain financial schemes and strategies without ensuring an adequate shared understanding by enough of the right people.

It is of equal importance to understand what the company is and what it is not. This sounds easier than it is. Often businesses deal with their *perception* of what the business is or what people want it to be, not what it actually *is*, and fall prey to blind spots, myths, or golden calves. One automatic data collection company Ed worked with had a large manufacturing component, making radio frequency wireless networks and mobile computer terminals. Manufacturing, under forceful leadership, persuaded the other executives that it was one of the core competencies of the business. Nothing was further from the truth. A number of alternatives to the manufacturing capability could have provided lower-cost and higher-quality products and/or services, but the group never explored them because it never questioned its own dead certain belief that manufacturing was the core value. The belief turned out to be deadly indeed: it led to more investment of time, effort, and dollars in manufacturing than warranted, and stifled investment in other areas—such as product development and marketing—that could have boosted growth, profitability and value to the shareholders. As already the French enlightenment writer and philosopher Voltaire observed, "Doubt is not a pleasant condition, but certainty is absurd."

If you're not stuck in your own past beliefs but open to a whole new way of doing things, you might come up with—or simply hear about—a revolutionary business idea. The most innovative companies have been willing, even eager, to travel the world in search of best practices, and then recombine them or apply them in novel ways to solve customer problems. Take Cemex, the Mexican cement company that became a world leader by using GPS to innovate its logistics infrastructure. The Cemex team that built the GPS-based on-time delivery system got the idea from a 911 call-center they saw in Houston. Since cement dries up quickly, they saw that contractors needed just-in-time delivery, and reckoned by analogy that an emergency response team faced the same issue of acting quickly on urgent requests from unpredictable sources. Based on this insight, they studied how the call-center dispatched paramedics within ten minutes despite traffic congestion and unpredictable call patterns.[51] GPS-based cement delivery was born. The idea revolutionized the industry and pushed Cemex into market leadership.

Later in the chapter you will see how you put all of this together in building your Strategy-In-Action; first we have to talk about how to moderate the process.

Rule 5: Get an Unbiased Facilitator

Case: Changing the BBC

In the 1990s, a reform-minded British Broadcasting Corporation executive named John Birt brought in the consulting firm McKinsey to reshape the BBC's ten-year strategy document.[52] Most of the consultants were freshly-minted MBAs who learned about the business while reengineering it. Strategy meant formally changing the processes by which the BBC worked: who reported to whom, what, and how often. The problem was that the consultants did not fully grasp the nature of creative work, so they tended to dismiss its value. They took little responsibility for implementing the changes they advocated, nor did they deal with the human ramifications, for example the results of shifting large numbers of people from areas in which they had developed expertise to others in which they were driving blind. After a year the consultants were paid, left the organization in turmoil, and increased social distances within the BBC—while increasing employees' feelings of anxiety dramatically.[53] The BBC fiasco is a typical example of what can happen when strategists impose solutions without first forging a shared understanding of all stakeholders.

McKinsey's own Richard Foster and Sarah Kaplan sounded the alarm to awaken corporate executives from the slumber of old unexamined assumptions. In their aptly titled book *Creative Destruction* they cited example after example of companies that suffered from "cultural lock-ins" and blind spots that produced "a collective failure of the mental processes"—for example the well-known case of IBM in the 1980s when personal computers swept the industry. Just like any human beings, corporate decision-makers find familiar facts comforting and explain away inconsistent data.[54] The longer the company has been in a particular business, and the larger the organization, the more habitual thinking and group-think can take over.

Not least for this reason, the CEO is as well served by using a facilitator to assist in Stategy-In-Action. Most CEOs are capable of moderating the process themselves; on occasion we have each done it with our own companies. But the do-it-yourself approach has its drawbacks. First, no matter how open the CEO is (or professes to be) to input, for most people he or she is difficult to challenge. Though we would all like to participate in the strategy process with our teams as equals, it is difficult for people to ignore that the CEO—with all the authority and power that comes with that title—is in the room. And it is near impossible to think "without scissors in your head," as one of our clients calls it, if the CEO is also facilitating the process. The CEO's facilitation, indeed his or her mere presence in the meeting, may shut people down.

Second, to maximize team inputs and creativity, the CEO or leader should be free to participate—or not to—in specific stages of the process. John F. Kennedy did this in the Cuban Missile Crisis: the president chose the right people to decode the strategic situation, then left the meeting at critical times to allow his whiz kids to hammer out a shared analysis of the situation. Similarly, we have found that it can be good sometimes for the CEO to use his or her absence to spur team creativity or a fresh look. We needed to completely withdraw from time to time to allow the other team members the room to contribute fully without feeling intimidated. You cannot do that if you are also the facilitator.

Third, the strategic process gives you the chance to observe key managers and frontline people in a unique work setting, get their views and vantage points, and see how they interact. You don't want the facilitator role to get in the way of listening, learning and gaining valuable insights. And lastly, while the CEO is entitled to his or her own opinions, the moderator is not (or not as much). Coupling the leadership role with the facilitator role may rob you of your own self-expression as a stakeholder in the process. Facilitating and leading are two distinct functions: If you facilitate, you must be impartial and the participants must believe that you are; you are not as free to voice your opinions. Such self-censorship might weaken your leadership unnecessarily. We think it's a good idea to split the roles of leader and facilitator. By choosing someone else to moderate the discussion, the CEO ends up getting more honest inputs.

Is it better to use a facilitator from within the ranks of the company or to hire an outside consultant? The decision depends in part on the capability within the strategy team. Is there someone in the organization the CEO meshes with and trusts to be an honest and impartial broker? The moderator must have a broad vision and the leadership skills necessary to facilitate the process effectively, check his or her ego at the door, reveal possible elephants on the table, call a spade a spade, put his or her own agenda aside, listen to all points of view, give voice and a fair shake to everyone on the team, and keep generating alignment. Last but not least, he or she must be willing to stand up to the CEO and speak truth to power.

Rule 6: You're Never Done

To achieve a truly shared understanding, the strategy team defines what exists today, warts and all. We like to talk about unvarnished truth: an honest and realistic baseline of what is and what is not (as opposed to what should be, which comes later). The shared understanding is a moving target that evolves throughout the process as the team gains more knowledge in other phases. As you implement your strategy, obstacles and details come up, and misunderstanding, dissent and fragmentation happen easily. The team might find itself going back to and adapting the shared understanding so that it remains true. In every phase of the process, shared understanding is needed newly for bundling the energies of your colleagues into a laser beam of alignment. A shared understanding is not an item you can tick off on your checklist, but something you create over and over again.

Shared Understanding: Precursors

Lets focus on practice and discuss how to get your Strategy-In-Action process up and running. You have chosen the strategy team, engaged an (internal or external) facilitator, and set up a framework for the shared understanding. That is merely the starting point. The team will need to understand the knowledge, as well as add, delete, spindle and mutilate it, until each participant is sure that all the key components are on the table. Taken together, this is a broad and comprehensive view of the organization today, including its market, its industry, and its environment. To accomplish that, you need to gather and analyze not only all relevant areas about the company, but also the knowledge about your competitors. Your own company data will probably be most reliable, the industry data a bit less so and the competitive data the least.

Three issues come up immediately. One, how do you get the team to be on the same page and to function as a team, rather than a group of individual players? Two, how do you get the team to think and act effectively in the strategic arena? And three, how do you get the underpinnings of a shared understanding into the team's hands so they can begin the Strategy-In-Action process?

Though many stakeholders may know each other at least in passing, they have rarely worked together as a team. Some will have limited experience with strategic processes. Some doers in the company may not place high value on strategy and the impact it can have on the company's future. They might be jaded from similar exercises in the past, especially if those processes did not yield desired results. And since you are taking strategy team members away from their important day-to-day work, but still hold them accountable for the results as if they were there, some might be outright frustrated about their new assignment.

One exercise that pulls the team together and shows the power of non-verbal communication is to have several breakout groups draw a picture. The assignment can be to draw any picture, or a more specific picture of the company (for example, one team Thomas worked with asked itself, What would our company look like if it were a boat?). The team is broken up into small groups of four. Each team member is given a marker. A flipchart page is placed in the center of each sub-team. The rules: nobody talks, each participant draws only one line at a time, they take turns and they draw something recognizable. Give them 15 minutes to draw the picture, then each breakout group presents its picture to the plenary. The intended results: team members start to get drawn into the process, they have fun, teammates get to know each other, and—perhaps most importantly—they think visually and interrupt their habitual language.

The second exercise builds on the first. The team is tasked to develop a company history with significant milestones. You take a roll of paper (or four flipchart pages in a row) three to four feet (about one meter) wide and some twelve feet (four meters) long. You tape it to the wall at shoulder level and draw a horizontal line along the middle of the paper. Now each team member takes a fat marker and puts up whatever he or she sees as key company milestones, writing his or her initials next to each milestone. There is no discussion, evaluation or censorship of ideas; all ideas are equally valid. When everyone has finished, starting from the most distant past, each milestone is discussed by the person who put it up,. The team can add new events out of the discussion. The expected outcome: the team gets a shared experience of the company's history that each member contributes to. This immersion exercise can take up one or several hours. Teams usually enjoy it and often want to keep the history timeline on the wall throughout the strategy process. It's worthwhile as a precursor of shared understanding and for deepening ownership of the organization.

Shared Understanding: Interviews and Whitepaper

You have two steps for getting at the underpinnings of a shared under-standing: interviewing key stakeholders individually and documenting the findings as a straw man in your kick-off meeting. Strategy-In-Action places a premium on hearing all views about all critical elements of the business. The goal is comprehensive alignment on what the business is and what it is not. The exploration needs to be broad and deep enough to address all business fundamentals. Make sure that each participant has total freedom to say what is on his or her mind, speculate, and express thoughts that might sound far-fetched or even stupid. Each interview needs a safe and confidential environment for the employee to respond truthfully, without fear of repercussions; and the ability for employees to engage in open discussions and ask questions without feeling they put themselves out on a limb.

In the interview process you face a basic trade-off. On the one hand, to safeguard full confidentiality and anonymity, it might make sense to use an external interviewer who is not loyal to anyone in the company, not biased, not blind to the company's taboos, and not beholden to its sacred cows. On the other hand, in his roles as chief executive, chief op-erating officer or general manager, Ed has often used a facilitator from inside or outside the firm, but he insists on conducting most interviews himself, across functions and levels, because it puts his hand on the pulse of the whole organization.

Since an extensive interview process can become a time sucker, with larger companies Ed uses a sampling technique: meetings with eight to twelve employees at a time. These group meetings are peers only—no su-periors or subordinates are invited. Ed aims to hold group meetings by function, but at times mixes functions to keep the peer rule. The results have been consistently good. Employees are closest to the customers and to the work. They know the issues, they know what works and what doesn't, what they would like to change, what customers want and what they see the company should be doing. We have found that employees are usually correct 90 percent of the time, at least. An employee may not know how to address an opportunity or how to fix something, but they know when an opportunity exists or when something is broken; they may not know how to manage a complex issue through the company to meet a customer need, but they know what that need is.

Whoever ends up doing the interviews, what matters is that each interview is face to face or at least over the phone, not merely on paper or through an online survey. This allows you to dig underneath their first answers by asking questions like, "Why? What exactly makes the marketing department strong? What's your evidence for saying that we focus too much on manufacturing instead of services?" and so forth. We keep detailed notes of what people say but do not attribute quotes to any individual. The interviews should be confidential and anonymous so that people have the freedom to say uncomfortable truths without fear of repercussions. People afraid of being ostracized or even fired will not say what they really think (would you?).

Whether you interview stakeholders individually or through group meetings, your questions come in three major components: what's so now (the current situation, including current results in key performance indicators, results by product or service area, key trends over the past three years, market signals, developments at key competitors, the current organizational culture, cultural taboos, significant events in the last year, and so forth)? What's missing for the future and what are the blockages that prevent the achievement of the company's desired future (for example, what are the chronic issues, what frustrates people the most)? And what are key opportunities (things that are already working on the periphery and/or on a small scale, and could point to the desired future)?

You can present your findings in a written interview report or a slide deck. This "Whitepaper" becomes the straw man the strategy team will vet. Make sure the Whitepaper does not let anyone see who said what in the interviews. Like the interviews, the Whitepaper entails three major components: What's so now? What's missing, what are the barriers in the way of achieving the future? And, What are the opportunities?

Component 1: What's So?

The "What's So" of your current situation comes in five areas. In some of them hard data will not be available; they are often the very areas in which companies or teams delude themselves, so the discussion should focus on what is real and what isn't, splitting facts from fiction or commonly held beliefs.

First, **industry and market data** are about the boundaries the company operates in, such as market size, market growth rates, competitors, substitutes or industry trends. The best topology we know for evaluating industries and markets can be found in Michael Porter's *Competitive Strategy: Techniques for Analyzing Industries and Competitors*[55].

Next is the company's **business model and value proposition**. You define not only your own, but if possible also the business model of each key competitor. The drivers of value creation are typically a combination of sales growth, operating margins, capital turnover, and cost of capital. Understanding these elements for the company and competitors helps assess the value-creation capacity in the whole system. For example, what drives your sales growth is your product development capability, the product's competitiveness, your pricing, marketing capability, and distribution strategy.

Third is a **financial analysis** to see how the company executes its business model, builds value, and positions itself against competitors. No shared understanding is complete without a financial analysis in four forms: the profitability and value based on the business model, the profit-and-loss statement, the balance sheet, and the cash-flow statement. If possible, the analysis should include not only financial data but also operating metrics, and go beyond reporting mere data to understanding what drives them: what is working, what isn't, and what is not being addressed at all. Your approach to the financial analysis will be slightly different from the rest of the process. Everything up to this point has been accomplished on a participative basis within the stakeholder team. By contrast, the financial analysis should be done before the shared understanding session and presented to the group by the chief financial officer, who then leads an interactive discussion on the ramifications of the analysis.

Fourth is the **internal analysis**. A simple tool for tying things together is the well-known SWOT (Strengths, Weaknesses, Opportunities and Threats) analysis. Relying upon the information gleaned so far, SWOT attempts to formulate the complete picture of the company and combines qualitative and quantitative analysis.

Last is an **organizational and cultural analysis** that focuses on the skill-sets—both existing and missing—and on cultural norms and taboos. Here you ask questions about organizational effectiveness such as: "Does the organization enhance or hinder the work needed?" or "Is the organization sized properly for the business and the industry?" The cultural analysis identifies the company's core values and how they impact organizational results. It ties culture to performance and looks for ways to improve both. It puts unwritten norms and rules on the table that might either be constraining or enabling performance.

Once you have gathered and analyzed the data, you and your strategy team should bundle all your findings so far into five to ten fundamental observations about what's so now.

Component 2: What's Missing? What Are the Blockages?

Once you have got your arms around what's so, you can ask, "what's missing?" This is not like asking, "what's wrong?" Far from it: what's missing is really another cut at what's possible. If you and the team ask what's missing long enough, you will sooner or later come up with leverage points for the future. Similarly the question, "what are the blockages?" pinpoints your attention on the barriers to the future. Just like what's missing, blockages are leverage points for clearing your path. When we facilitated a strategy session with key stakeholders at a multinational financial-services company, the participants came up with these statements of what's missing and key barriers:

- *Communication: Disconnect top vs. bottom. Lack of specific, empowering, useful and candid communication and skills. No understanding of strategy below top management (sequence of actions is unclear). No external communication.*
- *Culture: Cultural clashes not addressed. Lack of trust between cultures. No integrated, designed overall culture.*
- *Leadership: Missing unified and aligned leadership with commitment, ownership, and engagement. Lack of leadership at top. Low credibility of top management from employee's point of view.*
- *Priorities: No clear and target-oriented value proposition (what's in it for me?). Priorities unclear. Too many targets and priorities.*
- *Vision: Imprecise target state.*

And here is an example of a flipchart we generated with a medium-size high-tech defense manufacturer:

- *What's missing: Annual EBIT stems from 2 contracts. Unsystematic internal communication. Reactive not proactive. Balance of standardization vs. customization not strategic. No entrepreneurial culture (new products / markets / risks). No independent testing of product / personnel. Insufficient understanding of marketplace.*
- *Blockages: Legacy culture and business model focus on short-term vs. growth. No perceived company vision and strategy.*

Component 3: What Are the Opportunities?

We define "opportunities" as innovative activities happening at the organization's periphery and often ignored by top management, but consistent with the organization's mission, that point the direction to the future and could be scaled up or replicated elsewhere. Innovative ideas are seldom born at headquarters, where senior managers have little incentive to change the status quo. Why? Because they get much of their current power and perks from the way things have been and are now. They might see innovation as a subversion of the current order, or even as a threat. Far-flung areas are free from those constraints, so at times the strategy team has to look far and wide for opportunities that point to the future. At the high-tech manufacturer above, the team identified these opportunities:

- *Training & Development.*
- *Single group for T&D/Testing/Service.*
- *Military applications for use-of-force product.*
- *Application of standard product to expanded markets—public safety, utilities, transit / Para-transit / school buses.*
- *Move to relation/geographic sales model (i.e. leverage).*
- *Integrate up to 3 products w/ common scenarios.*
- *Railway Simulation.*
- *Entry-level products.*
- *Recurring revenues from warranties, up-sell.*
- *Convoy trainers.*

At the global financial-services company, the strategy group saw these opportunities for scale-up or replication.

- *Integration/Synergies: More than 6 months of integration. Starting and running global project. Global units within IT.*
- *Off-shoring/Outsourcing know-how: 3 years off-shoring experience, including change management. Use of existing locations and processes.*
- *Reorganization/Outsourcing: Outsourcing experience.*
- *Existing cross-cultural skills: Global orientation. Cross-cultural openness.*

Alignment vs. Agreement

Stakeholders come to the process with a range of people skills, strategic knowledge, organizational knowledge, personal relationships, and agendas. There will be different levels of commitment to the strategy process, types of experience, and levels of strategy skills. And as we said above, some stakeholders' desires to participate may not be in sync with those of others. Even if it's not all milk and honey, you want to encourage these differences throughout the process. The upside is that stakeholders look from their unique points of view and through their own filters. The facilitator's challenge is to harness those strengths while maintaining alignment on the strategy and on the process itself.

Strategy-In-Action is about gaining alignment, not agreement, which all too often devolves to a watered-down "consensus" or the lowest common denominator. You want much more: a team that is on the same page and pulls in the same direction with powerful unity. That does not mean everybody needs to agree on everything. In fact healthy dissent is a must for alignment and should be encouraged. Without doubt there is no chance for innovation, the physicist and Nobel laureate Richard Feynman once said; and as our colleague Peter Block puts it, without doubt there is no chance for authentic commitment.

You usually don't get alignment from voting either. The discussion must go on until all participants are aligned on all key elements. Alignment allows for dissent, but once the team has discussed all the options and arrives at the solution, participants are expected to support the alignment and move on. It is up to the facilitator to see when a critical mass of alignment is achieved and further discussion of an issue would mean beating a dead horse.

To keep the process moving forward efficiently, you can use a combination of approaches. You can utilize an "either/or" style to make choices clear, stark, and inevitable. Voting on alternatives can be a key tool in breaking an impasse on the path toward alignment. If you find yourself in a circular discussion, the facilitator may list the alternatives on a flipchart or on a slide you beam to the wall, which allows you to document and disseminate the conversation later and to build a shared knowledge base that validates your shared understanding. Each stakeholder gets several stick-on dots and votes on the alternatives they see as the priorities. The number of dots for each participant should fall short of the number of options. The number of dots each option receives gives you the priority listing.

You can break the strategy group into sub-teams that work on specific areas and bring them back to the plenary for key decisions only. The composition of these breakout teams is not random but by design. You can mix different disciplines and perspectives in each. Switch team compositions around so as to forestall groupthink. Have each breakout group name a team leader, and encourage team leaders to be interactive and give everyone a voice.

Lastly, in some cases you can rely on outside experts or end-users. To assist a global healthcare company in entering India and China with an innovative diabetes solution, Thomas and his fellow consultants from McKinsey involved several local experts who could provide crucial insights, and even interviewed local patients on video to be sure the shared understanding would include the views of end-users.

The process leader should be ready for surprises, disappointments and frustrations. On the other hand, great nuggets of knowledge and unknown synergies can surface too. You may be surprised at what the team knows and what it doesn't. Typically you will be impressed with the richness of data in some areas and appalled at glaring knowledge gaps in others. It takes patience in the early stages to knit it all together, take two steps backward for each step forward, challenge tribal beliefs, and seek new ways of looking at the company. But the potential rewards are great, both for the stakeholders and the organization.

The discussion is likely to highlight a number of disagreements or questions that call for more analysis or fact checking. As you develop your shared understanding, don't get bogged down arguing over the accuracy of specific facts (with the exception of the financial analysis, which is not subjective but simply has to be right). From a team-building perspective you want to encourage open debate and bold thinking. Once the straw man is at a point the team is satisfied with and nobody has anything critical to add, you can give assignments for additional research and fact-checking offline. Assign each open area to a team member, with a deadline for answering open questions and bringing the answers back to the plenary. You can reserve a flipchart page as a "parking lot" for open items, with the name of a stakeholder accountable for resolving them and the deadline for resolving each, so that nothing falls through the cracks.

The straw man is complete; all that remains for now is to write it up and distribute it to each participant. This matters, since sometimes people hear what they want to hear, and you want to be sure that the shared understanding is captured black on white. A crucial foundation of the strategy has been laid: the first cut of a multi-faceted understanding of the business, including internal and external factors. The team is ready to go to the next step that builds upon the work so far: creating the strategic vision and intent.

~

Boiling It Down

❏ The starting point of Strategy-In-Action is to forge a broad and unvarnished understanding of what the company is and what it is not.

❏ Six ground rules are most effective: #1: Make the team large enough to include all views, but small enough to be effective. #2: Tolerate dissent and doubt. #3: Bring back the big picture and create a context big enough for all points of view. #4: Confront the sacred cows (and calves). #5: Engage an unbiased broker to facilitate. #6: Manage Strategy-In-Action as a process, not an event or a task on your checklist.

❏ The vehicles for building the shared understanding are interviews, a whitepaper with a blind and anonymous executive summary grouped into key themes and issues, and a discussion in the strategy team. The key questions are, what's so? What's missing? What are the blockages? And what are the opportunities?

❏ An external analysis of industry and markets defines the boundaries and possibilities in which the organization operates.

❏ The internal analysis should consider five major components: organization, culture, SWOT (strengths, weaknesses, opportunities and threats) analysis, core competencies, and critical success factors.

❑ No shared understanding is complete without a financial analysis in four forms: the business model and how it drives profitability and value, the profit-and-loss statement, the balance sheet, and the cash-flow statement.

❑ Alignment is not agreement. People need not agree on all points, in fact they should disagree, but they must all pull in one direction.

CHAPTER FOUR

Which Gap? Strategic Vision and Intent

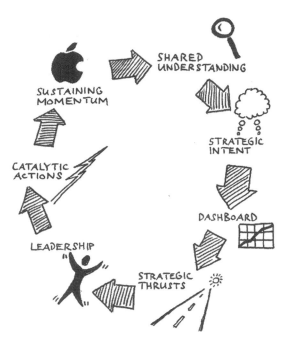

*Do you want to spend the rest of your life selling sugared water
or do you want a chance to change the world?*
—Steve Jobs to John Sculley (then at Pepsico)

In our mini-history in Chapter 2 about the birth of the Internet, we did
not mention several outlandish entrepreneurs who first envisioned the
medium and the world it might make possible. Take Jim Clark, who

pushed cyberspace before anyone else did. "One of the things that struck me at that early embryonic state," the founder of Netscape recalled, "was that the Internet was going to mutate the newspaper industry, was going to change the classified-ad business, and change the music business." Another visionary is Pierre Omidyar, a French-born Iranian computer programmer who founded eBay, said he did so "on the notion that people were basically good, and if you give someone the benefit of the doubt, you'll rarely be disappointed. I think what eBay has shown is that, in fact, you can trust a complete stranger."[56] Both Clark and Omidyar saw the future before others did, and both had the daring to stand in that future instead of the circumstances.

Visionaries like Clark and Omidyar are rare; regulatory pressures and the ever-present threat of lawsuits have made many executives and directors cautious. Many business leaders spend the overwhelming majority of their time merely managing what exists. (How much of your day do you spend on maintenance, managing the status quo, and running the business, versus working on the future, building, and *creating* the business?) Particularly in times of crisis, even the best are prone to revert back to what used to work before. How can you cast out a vision and build a future that is not a mere extension of yesterday's business-as-usual? That is the focus of this chapter.

One of the tenets of Strategy-In-Action is that strategists—indeed all managers—must create the future *from the future*, not from the past. You can be informed by the past; you can even respect and honor it; but you should never be enslaved by it. This chapter explores how to build strategic vision and strategic intent; how to ensure that your vision and intent are embraced by your stakeholders and owned as theirs; and how to stand in the future like the Omidyars and Clarks of the world—and others who have the boldness and daring to stand for a possibility larger than themselves, and mobilize their colleagues and contemporaries for that possibility.

Case: Kleiner Perkins—Betting on the Future

One company that sinks or swims based on its capacity to stand in the future is Kleiner Perkins Caufield & Byers. The venture capitalist has financed all kinds of promising ventures, including such stars as Netscape and Google, since 1972, and is about something bigger than making money: "solving the next huge problem for the planet," gushed one Kleiner partner, Randy Komisar.[57] And sometimes you bet on the wrong horse. Back in 2001, Kleiner partner John Doerr predicted Segway would be the fastest company in history to hit $1 billion in sales. Eight years later, it's not even close. "If you look out far enough," said Paul Kedrosky, a long-time observer of the venture capital industry, "I have no doubt that many of the bets will pay off. But in the venture business, being early is indistinguishable from being wrong."

For our purposes, what matters more than its batting average is how the company works. The ability to take bold risks that match the future is a product of Kleiner's culture, a mix of complementary talents that existed since its beginnings. In 1972, Eugene Kleiner, an engineer who had worked at the valley's first semiconductor companies, went into business with Tom Perkins, a former executive at Hewlett-Packard. Kleiner, who died in 2003, was an Austrian-born intellectual of modest tastes—"a very soft-spoken, very wise, very gentle man," according to Doerr—while Perkins was a brash gambler who would later build one of the world's most expensive yachts. "Tom would say, 'When you have a great opportunity, push all the chips, all the resources that you can, to the center of the table.'" Kleiner had the capacity to reflect, explore, and dwell in the future; Perkins was unafraid to take outlandish actions based on that future.

The complementarity of talents continued after the co-founder's death. One partner, Ray Lane, liked to divide his peers into technologists, who analyze the technical feasibility of ideas, and networkers, who help start-ups with their vast numbers of contacts in business, academia and politics. "I probably have 6,000 contacts in my Rolodex," said Lane, adding that he and Doerr have a friendly competition over who has more. The networkers include Al Gore and Colin Powell, who certainly don't hurt the firm's chances.

The Grip of the Past

Some of us might be skeptical of Kleiner's ventures and Clark's or Omidyar's bold ideas; and at this stage of the Strategy-In-Action process, you might face the same kind of doubt. If weathermen cannot forecast the weather, economists cannot forecast the economy and companies cannot forecast the next quarter earnings, how can your strategy team formulate an accurate vision for the future? The skeptics have a point; but we are not looking for a photograph, we are setting the compass. Another argument is more silent and more forceful. Whether it be that we are loath to leave our comfort zone, risk aversion, the pull of the past, resignation to the status quo, or simply the drift of the day-to-day: most people tend to resist change. Take the QWERTY keyboard, which is not exactly the most efficient way of arranging keys on a keyboard; yet for over a hundred years virtually nobody questioned the QWERTY standard. Or take photocopying: It's hard to remember now that when consumers in focus groups were first offered the concept, they roundly dismissed the need for copiers and told researchers they were satisfied with using carbon paper.[58] The grip of the past on our imagination is strong. "There are always two parties," Ralph Waldo Emerson wrote, "the party of the past and the party of the future; the establishment and the movement." The party of the past need not be the end-users; we have seen that at times the most powerful defenders of the status quo are the top managers. "The organizational pyramid is a pyramid of experience," said Gary Hamel, a visiting professor at London Business School. "But experience is valuable only to the extent that the future is like the past. In industry after industry, the terrain is changing so fast that experience is becoming irrelevant and even dangerous. Unless the strategy-making process is freed from the tyranny of experience, there is little chance of industry revolution."[59] Earlier, in their acclaimed *Harvard Business Review* article "Strategic Intent," Hamel and his mentor and colleague, the late C.K. Prahalad, had written: "A company's strategic orthodoxies are more dangerous than its well-financed rivals."[60]

Strategic Vision

How do you build a future from the future? The answer is, you align on a multi-year strategic intent that can serve as a stabilizer through conditions of uncertainty. Many years ago, Coca Cola's vision was for a Coke bottle within reach of every human being on the planet. Similarly, Nokia's strategic vision used to be, "Put the Internet in everybody's pocket." Microsoft's vision is to "Help people reach their potential." Disney's is to "Create shareholder value by continuing to be the world's premier entertainment company from a creative, strategic and financial standpoint." Gottlieb Duttweiler founded the Migros Cooperative, now the largest Swiss supermarket chain, in 1925 with five Ford Model-T trucks loaded with sugar, coffee, rice, macaroni, shortening, and soap—and a vision of scrapping traditional distribution structures to help society's poorer classes.[61]

Case: A Flash of Inspiration

Strategic vision can reveal itself in a flash of inspiration. Keith Waters, a later instigator of one of the virtual era's more curious and less sung revolutions, used to be a computer consultant. His wife Cathy, a used-book dealer, came home one day and complained how difficult it was to find particular out-of-print books. Basically the only way was to scuffle through the local used-book stores or pore through the thirty or so pages of A B Bookman, a weekly magazine that published lists of titles.[62]

That's when an idea sparked in Waters: why not create an Internet equivalent, a searchable database that would connect thousands of dealers instead of only a few, and list millions of books instead of thousands? And so in 1996 he founded Advanced Book Exchange, abebooks.com. To make a long story short, AbeBooks now lists more than 140 million books, with 50,000 to 100,000 added every day by thousands of book sellers in 50 countries who each pay a monthly subscription. It soon offered six regional websites in North America and Europe. In the process, AbeBooks transformed the used-book market from a decidedly unsexy industry into a commercial powerhouse by organizing and centralizing an extremely fragmented market of tiny, back-street sellers through the Internet.

In 2002 the founders were bought out by Hubert Burda Media of Germany, and in 2008 Amazon.com purchased AbeBooks. Amazon does not report its used book sales separately, but the category is thought to account for roughly a quarter of Amazon's sales.[63]

Whether it comes to you in a surge, as it did for Waters, or whether you build it painstakingly over months with key stakeholders, a strategic vision is a statement of what is possible to achieve, is worth achieving, and represents a new quality of life for all concerned. It states the venture's long-term aspirations. It declares what you want to do, why you want to do it and the benefits doing it will bring.

How do you build vision in the midst of daily emails, meetings, calls, demands, and other pressures, though? One answer is, don't delegate the future to specialists but make it everyone's job. When Marissa Mayer, now the head of Yahoo, was still Google's vice president of search products and user experience, she sat down most Fridays with a group of some 50 engineers and other employees to search for new ideas. Mayer, an intense, fast-talking manager, scribbled rapidly as the engineers raced to explain and defend the new ideas they had posted on Google's intranet. After no more than 60 minutes, six to eight new ideas were usually fleshed out enough to take to the next level of development. But what matters is that Google's brainstorming is not reserved for specialists. "We never say, 'This group should innovate, and the rest should just do their jobs,'" said Jonathan Rosenberg, senior vice president of product management. "Everyone spends a fraction of their day on R&D."[64]

That's important, since people may not be at their most creative when you ask them to be. "It's certainly not in the brainstorming meeting scheduled for 2.30," says Bill Duggan of Columbia Business School. If you ask people when they have their best ideas, Duggan says, the answer is often in the middle of the night, in the shower, or when they are stuck in a traffic jam. "When brainstorming works, it is when someone has brought an idea into the meeting"; the idea was not generated in the meeting, as often supposed. And it is ideas creation—or what he calls "strategic intuition"—that intrigues Duggan. Strategic intuition is not a vague feeling, nor a reaction, but a flash of insight that solves a problem you may have been pondering for months. So how do you teach yourself to be strategically intuitive? Duggan has come up with a four-step description of how strategic intuition works. To begin with, you store information over time in the "shelves" in the brain. Second, you relax or clear your mind—he calls it "presence of mind" (the most difficult part of the process, though this technique is often used in eastern practices like meditation or yoga). Then different pieces of information selectively move together in your mind to form a flash of insight. Fourth, resolution to act propels you forward.

The implications of Duggan's theory are that there is nothing new under the sun, which can be both unnerving and liberating, he said, citing Starbucks. The founders of the coffee shop chain acknowledge that the idea came to them in Italy over a cup of coffee in one of the many local espresso bars. Starbucks adapted that concept to the U.S. market and the rest, as they say, is history. So if a company has a problem to solve, one way to look at it would be to ask: has any other company in the world solved part of this problem? This strategy has been used to great effect at General Electric.

With a true sense of academic integrity, Duggan willingly concedes that his concept of strategic intuition is not new either. "I didn't invent it; I stole it" from Napoleon Bonaparte, France's most famous military leader, and from Carl von Clausewitz, who wrote the classic military strategy about Napoleon, *On War*. Napoleon had flashes of inspiration that Duggan calls Napoleon's glance, or *coup d'oeil*.[65]

Today, building a potent strategic vision means converging on the answers to three sets of questions. The first set relies upon the work done by your strategic team for the shared understanding (see Chapter 3). What is the unique and valuable position the organization wants to be in and is able to accomplish? What will achievement of this position mean for the company, the major stakeholders, and the company's environment? Why does achievement of this position matter to key stakeholders, the organization, and the environment?

The second set of questions is, what unique and meaningful benefits will the company deliver to customers? How do these benefits differ from other competitive products and services—including substitutes—these same customers can get elsewhere? Is this differentiation sustainable in the foreseeable future? If not, what is missing for sustaining this differentiation?

The third set is, what organizational values will guide the organization on its journey to its unique and valuable position? What are the guiding beliefs about market trends, key assets, or customers? Once you have found good answers to these question sets, you can condense your findings in a compelling strategic intent that mobilizes your stakeholders.

Managing the Strategic Visioning Process

Strategic visioning is far from most people's ordinary work. Some are intimidated by the task, they don't know how to do it, or they think they cannot do it. So the job of the CEO and/or facilitator is to get the team members out of their own way, free from the past, and open enough to build and embrace a future vision.

One vision exercise is what our colleague Nicholas Wolfson calls the "Wall Street Journal process." Imagine the date is five years from today. *The Economist* is writing a feature about your organization's success. Adopt the name of a reporter and write about the company or the department.

- What were your organization's results? Your accomplishments?
- What was unique about your company's approach or strategy, and what unique and valuable position is the company in?
- What value did your company and/or its products add, and to whom? What unique benefits do customers get from the company? How do these benefits differ from competitive and substitute products? How sustainable are these benefits?
- What do these achievements mean for the company, the employees, other stakeholders and the environment?
- What were your core values and principles, and how did you express them?
- What unique assets did your company take advantage of to

achieve success? What made your company effective? What made it well-known?

- What do your customers / colleagues / VIPs say about your organization?

A key tip for this exercise is that participants be bold and inventive, and that there be no censorship. Ask people to suspend their skepticism and avoid statements like, "we've already tried that three years ago." And by all means, do not get into the How at this stage. Rather, the mood is one of speculation: "What if...?"

The second option is to split the strategy group into functional teams. The makeup of these breakout groups is critical and should not be left to chance. If the aim is depth in specific functional or regional areas, the facilitator could build teams by function, such as product development, marketing, sales, etc. On the other hand, if the intended outcome is consensus or the resolution of conflicts between silos, cross-functional teams might work better.

In the functional option, each group envisions what its area (for example sales or quality) could look like in five years, for example by co-authoring the 5-year *Economist* article above. This allows each breakout group to vision within its comfort zone, and might even engender some healthy competition between groups. In the cross-functional option, participants volunteer for key areas such as global footprint, people power, product launches, operational excellence, standardization, or margins and profitability. We ask each sub-team to look out three to five years in their area, anticipate likely changes in markets, technologies and products, and estimate what impacts those changes may have on the company. Each group comes back and presents its article to the plenary. The expected results are twofold. Participants get experience visioning within areas they care about; and the team's elements might go into a vision statement or strategic plan. This exercise easily takes a few hours or could be done as an overnight assignment.

Once each breakout group has shown its five-year vision article, its members prepare a slide or flipchart with the top-level vision condensed from its article. They choose a spokesperson who presents the team's vision and leads the discussion in the plenary, which then—in real-time—distills the major building blocks of a shared company-wide vision on another flipchart or slide. For this condensation of the vision articles to be comprehensive, it works if the facilitator takes notes of key points in each vision article presented, and to ask all participants to listen for key points in each article that inspire them. The technology department at the global bank we mentioned earlier came up with these elements of a strategic intent:

- *Common framework for change*
- *Smooth transition / Efficiency*
- *Cultural differences are ok/respected / Operate in unity*
- *Excitement / Employees enabled to cope and lead through the change*
- *Premier IT organization where everyone wants to work / institutional pride*
- *Save CHF 509m / increase ROE / increase share price through integrating in a way that's better than our competitors did*
- *Full communication / flow of information*
- *Leadership / ownership*

No matter how you do it, the outcome is that you have changed the mindset from today (no, yesterday) to tomorrow. People have overcome their fears about creating the future from the future and are now standing in a new possibility not given by the past. Palpable aspects of what the future might look like have begun to emerge.

Strategic Intent

The next step is to boil your strategic vision down into a strategic intent, a crisp and concise statement that captures the imagination of all your stakeholders and leaves them emboldened to achieve it. Strategic intent is a magnet, a force field that pulls the present to the future of the strategic vision. It conveys your burning desire to change the world—much like the gauntlet Steve Jobs' threw to John Sculley at the start of this chapter—and to finish ahead of whoever else happens to play. In their article of the same name, Gary Hamel and C.K. Prahalad defined strategic intent as "... a [sustained] obsession with winning at all levels of the organization." It is the effect you want to have on your world, or the road you will take to your strategic vision. The strategic intent must be big enough to be visionary, yet short-term enough for stakeholders to wrap their arms around and be energized.

The strategic intent should be three to five years out into the future. To align on the strategic intent, the strategy team uses the same ground rules and dynamics used up to this point. Make sure each member has a voice in shaping the strategic intent, and do not declare alignment until every person in the room is aligned and there are no more "yeah, buts". We often split the plenary into two groups who each create a draft strategic intent in no more than fifteen words at their flipchart. Then we use a voting procedure where the plenary votes for one of these two versions as the standard from which to work. Once the standard is chosen, we write that into a slide that we beam onto the wall. Now each team member can make a proposal to change the wording, that proposal is discussed briefly, then voted up or down. We continue the procedure until no participant proposes any more changes. The key is to clearly split the proposals from the discussion of each, and the discussion from the voting on each. (Beware: the tendency in most groups is to mix proposals, discussion and voting in one soup of opinions.)

Case: Put the Internet in Everybody's Pocket

It's worth telling a fuller story about Nokia, which in 2013 was acquired by Microsoft, but in the 1990s did path-breaking work driven by its strategic intent to "Put the Internet in everybody's pocket." In those years Hamel, the co-author of the "Strategic

Intent" article above, was a frequent visitor at Nokia's Helsinki headquarters; Prahalad's and his idea held Nokia's senior management in thrall. Strategic intent was a new way for an ambitious company in a country like Finland to think about the future. Amid its restructuring, Nokia needed not strategic memos drafted at headquarters for the investment community, but strategic intent that would stimulate every employee. The language of strategic intent was not just about financial controls, things that Jorma Ollila, the company's CEO since 1992, knew thoroughly; numbers alone would never provide employees with a future that would earn their personal commitment.

Kari Kairamo, CEO from 1977 to 1988 and chairman from 1986 to 1988, when he took his own life, had given the company the vision of being a telecom leader; his successor Simo Vuorilehto had taken it away; Vuorilehto's successor Ollila and his peers brought it back. Strategic intent provided a clear direction for employees and justified focused investments, yet granted flexibility about the means of getting to the future. It did not shun orchestration but left room for improvisation. This was the kind of language that Nokia's executives wanted to hear.

True strategic intent implies a sizable stretch for an organization. In the early 1990s, Nokia's existing capabilities and resources fell short, forcing the company to be more inventive and making the most of limited assets. There was an extreme misfit between Nokia's resources and its aspirations. This was not by accident but by design: It was Nokia's new strategic intent itself that *created* the mismatch. Nokia purposefully used strategic intent to define a fundamental challenge and stretch the organization into becoming a focused cellular leader.

Strategic intent should be simple and short so that it sticks; but the key is ownership, not length. The concise strategic intent proposed by Hunger Project experts—to "end chronic, persistent hunger in India"— did not sound quite right to the participants at the Delhi joint strategy session co-hosted by India's planning commission and THP. More to the point, it did not inspire them or call them to action. Instead, they aligned on a strategic intent that expressed their hero Gandhi's vision for all human beings to live in dignity and self-reliance: "Achieving the threshold: The chance for all our people to lead healthy and productive lives in harmony with nature." To most people this may sound a bit flowery, especially in the West and especially if they are used to a short and snappy strategic intent like "Beat Xerox" (Canon's strategic intent) or "Beat Benz" (the rallying cry of a Japanese carmaker); but it spoke to the culture of India and galvanized the people who needed to implement the strategy.[66] And the word "threshold" allowed for measurable indicators to determine India's progress in achieving its strategic intent; but that's another matter we will leave for the next chapter. First we have to set some ground rules for building strategic vision and intent.

The ROI of Co-Creating Vision

In their 1987 book, the late C.K. Prahalad and Yves Doz wrote that "a firm's strategic intent allows it to think of resources and competitive advantages differently and deploy them with greater imagination."[67] Interestingly, their definition treated the company as an "it" and made no mention of employee involvement. In this view, strategic intent is based on the CEO's "superior foresight." Charismatic leaders may feel they can create the vision themselves and sell people on their ideas later, once the vision is fully cooked. After all, isn't that what leaders do, or should do?

When Ed was at Lear Seigler early in his career, he learned a fundamentally different approach. The man who hired him was the late Stan Wasiuk, whose mantra was that "anything the mind can conceive it can achieve." That is one of the tenets of Strategy-In-Action. At the risk of repeating ourselves: your stakeholders will be much more likely to achieve a vision they have a hand in conceiving. The inverse is just as true: they will have difficulty owning and implementing a strategy they did not help build. Much like in the shared understanding phase of Strategy-In-Action, a CEO will see at least five strong advantages to a participative process. First, company employees and other stakeholders will be much more supportive of a vision they have co-created; they will take more ownership and accountability—even if it's the very same vision the boss might have built all alone. In short, you won't have to sell the vision later on because the stakeholders own it from the outset.

The second benefit bears repeating too: employees and other key stakeholders have much to contribute, if for no other reason than that ten heads are better than one. They may have access to how things really are, to fresh ideas or to market intelligence hidden to the boss. For a CEO to see strategy as his or her exclusive purview and to ignore other inputs smacks of arrogance and could be a sign of a much bigger blindness within the organization.

Third, one byproduct of the co-design process, alignment, is itself a highly valuable asset. Many CEOs ultimately lose their positions because they fail to achieve and maintain alignment—more than for any other reason. A participatory design process is a major vehicle for the CEO to gain alignment among the Board, executives and employees.

Fourth, a participatory design process has a better shot at matching the company's strategy and its employees' aspirations. As Hallstein Moerk, Nokia's former Executive VP Human Resources, put it, the telecom keeps "making sure that our associates' life strategies coincide with our corporate strategy and vision."[68]

Finally, in a non-participatory process the leader will have to go through an extended process of negotiation on objectives, measures and expectations later on. If the objective is to create highly effective strategic and operational performance, joint creation is the best basis for boosting productivity. Upon achieving alignment, participants can move swiftly from strategic intent to individual goals, with little or no need for negotiation or pep talks because the key players are already aligned and understand strategic intent at a depth that comes only through shared design. This will be most apparent when unanticipated problems arise, or when stakeholders have to make their own tactical decisions based on the strategic intent, as is now the case in the military. Top-down decisions are simply not good enough for fighting terrorist networks. In so-called net-centric warfare, airmen now have to call airstrikes from the field, and soldiers on the ground have to call tactical decisions on their own. The more the troops can own the bigger picture, the more likely their decisions will match the strategy instead of sabotaging it. The same is true for any virtual organizations whose members rarely see each other.

These are just five facets of the ROI of co-creation. Yes, Strategy-In-Action may take a bit longer than top-down approaches, but given its dynamism, you may be surprised at the creativity of your team and the flood of new ideas streaming forth once you give your colleagues a voice.

In building a truly shared strategic vision and intent that will be embraced by all stakeholders, three ground rules should be kept in mind. One, avoid judging emerging ideas, and refrain from even evaluating them. At the vision stage there are no smart or stupid ideas; all are equally valid. Avoid censorship and make sure that every stakeholder can express ideas freely—even schemes that may seem wild and crazy, without going prematurely into the "how" of feasibility.

Two, avoid group-think. Merely saying "Let's think outside the box" does nothing to encourage ingenuity. In fact a study showed that employees see the phrase "outside the box" as among the most inane and depressing in corporate jargon.[69] Instead, the facilitator must make sure that the conversation for vision and intent stays free of resignation or cynicism that stem from past experience. "This failed before" is not a phrase you want to hear at the vision stage. You can honor the past, but don't be a slave of the past. The opportunity is to build a future from the future.

The third ground rule is to keep the end-user in mind and to stand in his or her shoes. Mahatma Gandhi, whose strategic vision led to India's independence, said it this way: "Recall the face of the poorest and weakest man whom you may have seen, and ask yourself if the step you contemplate is going to be of any use to him. Will he gain anything by it? Will it restore him to a control over his own life and destiny? In other words, will it lead to freedom for the hungry and spiritually starving millions?"[70]

When you build your vision, it's easy to forget the end-user and stay in your own ivory tower. DaimlerChrysler's former chairman Jürgen Schrempp imposed his vision "Nur das Beste" (Only the Best) onto the joint company, with hilarious consequences. Mercedes cars became famous for their coffee cupholders that had obviously been designed with top quality standards but without the customer in mind: they were mostly useless as most cups spilled or wouldn't fit.

Standing in the shoes of the end-user sounds good, but actually doing it takes extra work and cannot be taken for granted. When Thomas worked with the global healthcare company above (jointly with McKinsey consultants, we mentioned this briefly in the previous chapter) on its strategy for entering China and India with its cutting-edge diabetes product, some fifty senior global managers of the company flew into the Singapore strategy meeting and did their homework: they heard presentations by health professionals from both target markets, and watched videos of Indian and Chinese patients with diabetes in an effort to come up with a strategy that would work locally. Still, when the assembled managers put their strategic intent for China on a flipchart, their draft intent was centered in the J&J corporate headquarters: it spoke of the company's productivity and profits, not of the lives it would touch and the difference its product would make in China. Even after a participatory strategy process, they were not standing in the shoes of *all* stakeholders. Thomas reminded the strategy group of the J&J Credo created in 1943 by Robert Wood Johnson who guided the company from a small, family-owned business to a global enterprise with 116,200 employees. The Credo that became a Harvard Business School case study begins with the pledge: "We believe our first responsibility is to the doctors, nurses and patients, to mothers and all others who use our products and services. In meeting their needs everything we do must be of high quality." Once the managers heard their treasured Credo, they reframed their strategic intent from the point of view of their target audience in China and came up with a strategic intent that could have just as well been written by a Chinese doctor and/or diabetes patient. The question is always, Will the strategic intent truly inspire all your stakeholders to own it as theirs?

Obstacles to Being Strategic

This example shows that a participatory process is no walk in the park; a number of obstacles can get in the way. First, organizations like to *talk about* being strategic but not all walk the talk: What they emphasize, encourage and reward is for the most part functional expertise, effective execution and business-as-usual. Getting people to go beyond their individual jobs and think on a broader spectrum can be a challenge.

Second, being strategic can take years of training, and is often the fruit of having held various roles that broadened your perspective. Some large companies systematically provide multi-faceted experiences—General Electric routinely rotates high-potential managers around functions and cultures for multiple vantage points on the company—but many managers' experience comes from only one silo.

Third, the visioning approach can meet with skepticism and pushback, especially in cultures that have been burnt by grand schemes. Take Germany ever since Hitler's vision of world domination led to a world destroyed: after World War II, German leaders shied away from any grand pronouncements. The country's former chancellor and revered elder statesman Helmut Schmidt liked to quip that people who need a vision should see an eye doctor. Even without such pushback, projecting the future is difficult, and forecasts by prized pundits for a mere few months can turn out wrong. But once your strategy group is able to bring the future to life as an aligned vision and strategic intent, it is ready to move to the next phase—measuring its achievement.

~

Boiling It Down

❑ **Strategic vision is a statement of what is possible to achieve, worth achieving, and a new quality of life for all concerned. It conveys the purpose of the company, its long-term aspirations, and the effect you anticipate having on your environment, on your world. It states what you want to do, why you want to do it, and the benefits that doing it will bring.**

❑ **Before aligning on the company's vision, you must stand in the future. Organizations and their managers are often in the grip of the past or current circumstances, which are by necessity an extension of the past. You cannot build a future from the past—all you get is more of the same.**

❑ **Strategic intent is a magnet, a force field that pulls the present irresistibly to the future. It implies a sizable stretch for the organization, even a strategic mismatch between its intended future and its current resources or capabilities. The strategic intent must be vast enough to be visionary, yet short-term enough for each participant to wrap his or her arms around it and to be energized into action. The sweet spot is usually three to five years.**

❑ Effective and fun visioning methods are to break the plenary into sub-groups and have them each write a five-year vision article about accomplishments, core values, differentiators, satisfied customers, and the value added to the community.

❑ The three ground rules for the vision stage are: Don't evaluate ideas or their feasibility; avoid group-think, resignation, skepticism, and cynicism; and stand in the shoes of the end-user.

❑ Shared vision is vastly superior to unilateral vision (see the story about Nissan vs. DaimlerChrysler). Alignment maximizes ownership, yields better intelligence, enhances right actions and self-reliance of middle managers and frontline people, is a valuable asset in and of itself, and takes less cajoling and persuasion later.

CHAPTER FIVE

The Art of Measurement: What's on the Dashboard?

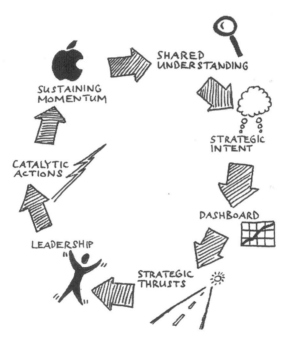

*Everything should be made as simple as possible,
but not simpler.*
—Albert Einstein

Charles M. Schwab, the late-19th-century U.S. industrialist who became by today's standards a billionaire in the steel industry, wrote in his memoirs that one day a century ago, before the night shift came in, he walked the factory floor and asked a workman for a piece of chalk.

> "How many heats has your shift made today?" I queried.
>
> "Six," he replied.
>
> I chalked a big "6" on the floor, and then passed along without another word. When the next shift came in they saw the "6" and asked about it.
>
> "The big boss was in here today," said the day men. "He asked us how many heats we had made, and we told him six. He chalked it down." The next morning I passed through the same mill. I saw that the "6" had been rubbed out and big "7" written instead. The night shift had announced itself. That night I went back. The "7" had been erased, and a "10" swaggered in its place. The day force recognized no superiors. Thus a fine competition was started, and it went on until this mill, formerly the poorest producer, was turning out more than any other mill in the plant.[71]

Such is the power of measurement. And that is what this chapter is about. The most stirring vision will come to naught unless all key stakeholders have aligned on a dashboard of clear, transparent indicators. If you don't know exactly where you are, it will be near impossible to get where you want to go. On the other hand, skillful measurement can enhance performance through friendly competition, targeted behaviors or strategic change. In this chapter we explore effective measurement systems, pitfalls to watch out for and obstacles to overcome, and tools for designing key performance indicators that align with your strategic vision and intent—not the past—and that pull for decisive, high-leverage actions by your teams. We will begin with a case where measurement has been particularly elusive: television.

Case: Measuring Television

For the last generation, watching television in America was defined by the families recruited for Nielsen Media Research who agreed to have an electronic meter attached to their TV or to record in a diary what shows they watch.[72] But in early 1992, a Maryland company called Arbitron took a distinctly unorthodox approach to measuring audiences. Arbitron's top managers called in their chief engineer, Ron Kolessar, and asked him: could he come up with a less expensive way to measure television and radio audiences at the same time? And make the measurements better too?

Until then, companies had been trying to collect data about U.S. television viewers by monitoring the set. The problem was, the more volunteers had to do to actively chronicle their program choices, like pushing a button or writing something in a diary, the less exact the information about the audience would be. And for years, both Nielsen's and Arbitron's ratings depended on selectively recruited Americans who usually got between $2 and $15 to fill out weekly paper diaries in hundreds of local media markets around the United States. These diaries were a very active form of measurement, subject both to errors of memory (you forget that you stopped on the Weather Channel for four minutes while flipping to another program) and to the human proneness to champion personal or habitual favorites (you write down "Mad Men" even if you were out of town that night). A diary cannot reliably measure what a person watched or listened to. It measures only what the person *says* he or she did.

This "active vs. passive" distinction matters. That's why in the late 1980s Nielsen first began to switch to a new electronic meter, the People Meter, which automatically notes what channel a TV is tuned to, and can also register who watches, as long as each viewer presses a log-in button. This gave Nielsen (and in turn,

TV programmers and advertisers) a wealth of new information. Thanks to the company's elaborate recruitment techniques, which included interviews and surveys of every prospective household, Nielsen could match the shows each viewer watched to his or her income, age, and ethnicity.

Kolessar briefed his team and went to work. When he finally presented the findings to Arbitron's executives, he suggested that the company go even further in passive metering than Nielsen's People Meter. No button-pushing, in other words. Here was the breakthrough in thinking: "We need to monitor the person," Kolessar declared.

After several years of painstaking and often frustrating development, Kolessar and his team came up with a coding that allowed for passive measurement. In Arbitron's view, encoding is the only plausible way to follow a piece of content to see if—and how—it reaches an individual. "Media is following you not just when you consciously turn on your satellite radio in your car," said Arbitron's CEO Steve Morris, "or when you consciously flip open your cellphone and get some cable channel delivered to it. It's also coming at you at the malls, where the L.E.D. screens are all around you along with the piped-in music. Advertising is becoming incredibly ubiquitous, so you need measurement that is equally ubiquitous."

Arbitron recruited a couple of thousand volunteers— men, women and children—in Houston and asked them to wear a black plastic box that looked like a pager, three inches by two inches by half an inch, whose circuitry is roughly as complex as that of a mobile phone. In the radio and television industry, this little box is known as a portable people meter, or PPM. In terms of business and culture, it also seems to be the equivalent of a large explosive.

Why such a little gadget should matter much to anyone beyond East and West Coast media elites may not be immediately obvious. But one indisputable fact about media measurement is that if you change how you count, funny things happen. Finding out whether "C.S.I." beats "Desperate Housewives" is just the beginning. Change the way you count, for instance, and you change where advertising dollars go, which in turn determines what shows are made and what shows are then renewed. Change the way you count, and potentially you change the comparative value of entire genres (news versus sports, drama versus comedies) as well as entire demographic segments (young versus old, men versus women, Hispanic versus black). Change the way you count, and you might revalue the worth of sitcom stars, news anchors, and—when a single ratings point can mean millions of dollars—the revenue of local affiliates and networks alike. Counting differently can even alter the economies of entire industries, should advertisers discover that radio or the Web is a better way to get people to know their brand or buy their products or vote for their political candidates. Change the way you measure your country's culture consumption, in other words, and you change your country's culture business, and maybe even the culture itself. Ultimately, what and how you measure determines how you and others see reality.

Just as important is what you *don't* measure. Even traditional TV channels reach a lot of viewers outside their homes. Take CNN or a financial news station like CNBC, which likely have large blocs of unmeasured viewers watching at work or at airports throughout the day. "Nielsen does not measure offices," Alan Wurtzel, head of research at NBC Universal, said. "Nor do they measure vacation homes. They don't measure hotels. They don't measure hospitals."

In addition, there's "time-shifting"—which happens when viewers rely on video-on-demand or TiVo-like devices (also known as digital video recorders or DVRs) to "shift" the times at which they watch their chosen programs. If a Nielsen family watches "Dateline" from its DVR three days after its broadcast, in other words, those viewers are not counted, and NBC gets no credit. Which may seem like a minor thing, except 31 percent (65 million) American households already had these devices by mid-2009.[73]

In 2005, Kolessar at Arbitron began tinkering with radio frequency identification (RFID) that would allow a Portable People Meter to track a reader's interaction not only with electronic media, but also with newspapers or magazines. A tiny chip embedded in a page, perhaps the size of a pencil dot, would tell a PPM that a reader picked up or opened a paper or magazine. PPMs might even register whether a majority of readers continued to the end of an article or stopped early. "We've got all sorts of things we're playing with in preparation for a world that is probably a couple years away," Kolessar said. "But it's going to happen. And it's going to happen because the advertisers are pushing this. It's them. They want to know more."

The Do's and Don'ts of Measuring

The case of measuring television allows us to distill some principles and best practices for why, what and how (including how often) to measure—all questions to be considered carefully, since the answers carry intended and unintended consequences. Above all, if you choose the wrong indicator or measure incorrectly, execution may be jeopardized. The top-level measurement system for your strategy implementation should be prototyped, if possible, at this stage of the strategic process.

There are many books on measurements, benchmarks, and dashboards—and more than a few consultants. Our goal is not to duplicate what you can easily learn from those sources. Instead, we want to explore the KPIs you need to execute successfully. Call us nitpickers, but in several decades of strategy work, Ed has never gone into a company that had a good measurement system at the outset. Typically such systems are cobbled together from existing disparate structures, behind the curve, and incapable of delivering the data and frequency you need. One technology startup launched a highly focused effort around a single product line. The financial and IT systems were designed to support that effort. Four years later the company decided to add a second product line. They launched the product, only to realize that there was no product-specific data available in the financial and IT systems because management had never given thought to the IT and Finance data needed for multiple product lines. Fixing this came at an enormous cost. This is an all-too frequent occurrence. It is better to know the state of affairs when going in so you can either do something about it or choose to live with a past-based system.

First you have to choose *whether* to measure anything; then you choose *what* to measure—outcomes as well as processes—to achieve the strategic intent. This is easier said than done. You can't measure everything. First, measurement isn't free. Collecting, reporting, and analyzing data costs time and money. From design to set-up and maintenance, the costs of a systems platform, storage and retrieval systems, report-writing tools, data warehouses, application software, and the middleware to connect it all can be significant. Second, if you measured everything, your measurement system would not highlight what is important. And third, unless you select systematically and deliberately what to measure, you have the potential of overwhelming the organization and sending it down the wrong path.

So why go through all that trouble? Here is why: the dashboard can make the difference between a good company and a great one. One benefit is that measuring itself affects improvement; measurement can bring focus or attention to specific areas. Nokia kept measuring phone size, cost of assembly, global availability of the GSM standard, and of course the number of customers as a critical path for its strategic intent to put the Internet in everybody's pocket. In China, the Finnish telecom invested in new computer systems that provided detailed sales data. "Tomorrow,

I will be able to tell you what happened today in the top 4,500 outlets," boasted Colin Giles, then manager of Nokia's China handset business, who would later become its global head of sales. "In a week's time, I will be able to tell you about 30,000 outlets."[74] Measurement can help monitor operations in areas as diverse as marketing, product development or customer relations; as CEOs we have often used metrics as the basis of coaching and performance management. And like the proverbial canary in the coalmine, measurement can serve as an early-warning system in revealing problems, finding solutions, and prevent nasty surprises.

But strategists should watch out for perverse incentives. The Dutch ministry of transport, public works and water management set itself an ambitious target by 2010: to reduce road fatalities to 750 and hospitalizations due to road accidents to 17,000. To achieve these goals, the ministry decided on a zero-tolerance rule. No more turning a blind eye to traffic violations or people throwing coke bottles out of car windows. The indicators (the number of violators apprehended) worked nicely and consistent with the goals—until it dawned upon the ministry that the unintended consequences of the zero-tolerance policy (for example overcrowded courts, unhappy voters) were worse and more costly than the original violations the policy was designed to deter.[75] So answering the "measure what?" question carefully is far from a useless exercise.

Case: Getting the Right Metrics for Life and Death

Perhaps we can learn something about how measuring progress on a vast strategic intent from the field of international development, one of the most complex human endeavors in history. When THP was founded in 1977, no one knew the extent of world hunger. This may sound strange today, when international data on chronic hunger are relatively abundant; but then, the global community had only vague estimates, if any, of how many people were living with and/or dying from hunger. This lack of facts made it extremely difficult to have leverage on the problem. It is the same with any endeavor: unless you know precisely where you are and how far you have to go to the finish line, you will be mired in a soup of uncertainty—you won't know whether your actions are enough or even right. Try winning a tennis game without keeping score; planning a family dinner without knowing when or whether people will be home; let alone building a business without knowing your numbers. By contrast, knowing precisely where we are brings out the best in us. Certainty gives us confidence, authority, and energy. It gives us a solid place to stand and a springboard to leap from.

So one of the first tasks THP undertook was to measure the scope of the problem. Roy Prosterman, then a professor at Texas A&M University, came up with an estimate of 41,000 individuals on average dying daily from hunger or hunger-related causes. But that number was impossible to observe directly. So in the late 1970s THP and its scientific advisers settled on an indicator of development measured annually by several UN agencies: the infant mortality rate (the number of babies per 1,000 live births who die before their first birthday). The IMR is widely considered a rough but useful benchmark of economic well-being and overall societal welfare since it not only reflects the health status and nutrition of young children and pregnant mothers, but has much wider significance. Infants die for a wide range of reasons, so the measure is also affected by such factors as racial disparity, access to adequate and safe food and drinking water, a country's health policy, air pollution, sanitation, shelter, vector-borne diseases, and environmental health management—not to speak of wars, two-thirds of whose victims are estimated to be children (about 500,000 children died as a result of the civil war in Angola alone). As THP's then-president Joan Holmes was to put it later:

> Hunger is humanity's oldest and most tragic problem. 35,000 of us a
> day die of the persistence of hunger. Three quarters of these deaths

are children under the age of five. Every minute of every day, 18 children die needlessly as a consequence of hunger. Imagine one hundred jumbo jets each filled with 260 children. Now imagine those 100 jumbo jets crashing. Hunger kills that many children each and every day. We don't build memorials to remind us but the number of people who have died of hunger and starvation in the past five years is more than all of those killed in World Wars I and II combined.

The organization's researchers soon ascertained that the IMR worldwide was 103, meaning that more than ten percent of all newborns died within their first year. Now THP had a yardstick for its strategic intent: the end of world hunger as measured by an IMR of 50 or below in every country.

By 2008, thirty years later, thanks to the efforts of hundreds of organizations, average incomes worldwide had more than doubled, life expectancy had increased by one-third, birth rates had dropped twenty percent, rural families with access to safe water had gone from ten to sixty percent, food production per capita had increased—and the average IMR worldwide had dropped to 49 per thousand infants.[76] (An IMR of 50 or lower will remain a dream for some time in Africa, a continent ravaged by AIDS, war, and political and economic turmoil, as well as in Afghanistan, with an IMR of 152.[77])

Traditional ways of measuring—for example per-capita income or the number of wells or hospitals or schools—are not only insufficient to the challenge but might actually be counterproductive because they lead to the wrong policy prescriptions that keep resource-poor people down and lead to more, not less, hunger. Holmes put her finger on why traditional measurements rarely work. "The methodology for scientifically valid assessment in the international community is developed for top-down, service-delivery strategies," she charged. "We need to stay committed to measuring and evaluating what we do—instead of distorting our programs to do what we can measure."[78]

What you measure is likely to run your and your people's lives. One of the measurement systems with the most impact in any company is the sales compensation plan that outlines clearly under what conditions and how much a salesperson will be paid for a sale. Companies design sales compensation to meet goals, including revenue goals, product goals and service goals. Count on it: within 24 hours of receiving their sales compensation plan, each member of the sales force has mined the compensation system for how they can make the most money with the least effort. All too often the corporate objectives and the salesperson's objectives are at odds with one another because the incentives are rigged poorly. The lesson again: beware of unintended consequences.

Once the "what" question is answered, you can move to the "how." The strategy team will want to check the process-level integrity of all benchmarks. How do the combined individual benchmarks perform as a system? Are all critical components being measured? Are any indicators redundant, given your strategic intent? What about the likely quality of the data? Is it sufficient to support the decision being made? A life-and-death decision needs more accurate data than a decision on which supplier to use (usually).

And how frequently should measurement happen? Those involved in the activities measured should have access to the data more frequently than those to whom they report. If the CEO and CFO look at data once a month, their direct reports might do so weekly. Those being monitored might look daily. They should build the measurements into their management routines and own the measurements as theirs. The bottom line: by answering the "why, what, how, and how often?" questions, the strategy team—or a task force within it—can run a cost/ benefit analysis before designing the measurement system and avoid unnecessary sunk costs.

Five Types of Metrics

As part of the How of measurement, the team should consider five types of metrics: strategic, operational, financial, competitive, and program/project. The five sets of indicators may overlap at times, but it is useful to look at each separately.

Strategic Indicators. Strategic metrics, the highest order of measurement, measure the results of a strategic objective or action. The key word is results, not processes or even effects or consequences. For a simple example, if the objective is efficiency, a KPI would be revenue per employee as opposed to mere revenue or profits. In R&D, a high-tech company might measure revenue from products no older than eighteen months, as opposed to meeting project targets only. At the simulation division of a military contractor we worked with, the team wanted to measure quality and aligned on two KPIs: first, the percentage of repeat business relative to total revenue (to measure the loyalty and sustainability of customers), and second, the number of service tickets vis-à-vis the time of purchase (to measure quality and customer satisfaction). The metrics for innovation were the percentage of R&D expenses against overall expenses as well as the number of new patents filed.

In designing strategic indicators, the first step is to revisit the desired outcomes stated in the strategic vision and intent. What will success in three to five years from now look like? The second—often more difficult—step is to find indicators for those results and accomplishments. What works best is to first brainstorm all possible measurements—without censorship, judgment or skepticism—and list them first before evaluating them one by one. As tempting as they are, qualitative measurements alone will likely yield disappointing results. Far better to go through the harder search for quantitative indicators and select the metric that most closely measures the desired outcome.

Financial Indicators. The second type of metric is familiar to most planners. Financial metrics provide black-and-white feedback of economic value and performance; they are generally accepted standards; and practices for collecting, recording, and reporting financial data are widespread. Key high-level data are typically reported in three standard formats: the Profit-and-Loss (P&L) statement, the Balance Sheet, and the Cash Flow statement. Often a company's financial systems meet accepted reporting standards but are not suited for measuring strategic or operational results. For example, the organization might have good data on its overall gross margin, but little or none on specific product, region or customer margins. How can that be? Perhaps a company that started out with a single product has evolved to multiple products but neglected to update its financial reporting to reflect the expansion. When Thomas worked with an energy company's downstream retail team on its strategic intent to earn 1 Euro more per customer in its shop operations, at the time of the strategy creation, the company produced 3 Euro per customer and wanted to expand that to 4 Euro. The condition for satisfaction was to achieve the strategic intent not through selling more gas, but solely through product sales at the shops and kiosks in gas stations. With some 80 million customers, that came to some 80 million Euros additional revenue. This was easier said than done, since the company had sold petrol exclusively through a network of independent gas station operators and was not set up for managing complex shop inventories. The retail team had to come up with new systems to measure data on sales of pastries, sandwiches, magazines, sunglasses, or auto supplies.

When data is compressed for efficient collection and reporting, it can be difficult and expensive to disaggregate to measure new products or trends. Other times financial reporting is not integrated, so the company has not one but multiple systems, for example one for compensation, one for manufacturing and one for customer care, forcing strategists to deal with a thicket of different sources, data definitions, and reporting times. Typically reporting happens monthly, quarterly and annually, but that routine can be at odds with having decision data available on an as-needed basis, since data collection supports the month-end close and other financial cycles rather than strategic or operational decision-making.

Operational Indicators. Operational indicators are non-financial quantitative metrics for monitoring performance. Ideally they serve as canaries in the coalmine to anticipate problems before they become crises. They show the health of the organization's key processes for achieving its strategic intent. Operational benchmarks can yield a wealth of utility: from getting your hands on the levers and dials of the business to understanding its value chains, they serve to monitor, report status, identify gaps, and predict results for higher-level indicators. To design them, the team breaks each strategic indicator and each value chain into key building blocks: functions, activities, and tasks. For each process and each KPI, the team defines who needs to know what and when.

Competitive Indicators. Benchmarking against the competition is essential for intelligence that goes into the ongoing strategy and for gauging the organization's impact in the marketplace. In its early days, AOL pushed its membership in direct competition to Microsoft's MSN. AOL's marketing director Jan Brandt was so obsessed with the number of members as a competitive benchmark that she used her car's license plate for AOL's fight. It read "2MILL" for two million customers. (Once AOL had passed that milestone, she changed the license plate to "FG8S"— for "F--- Gates.")

To develop the right competitive KPIs, it can be helpful to describe the organization in terms of industry standards available off the shelf, which saves you the cost and effort of reinventing the wheel by compiling industry data. But there can be good reasons for a non-standard industry definition, for example if the company is in an emerging industry, if the industry is evolving quickly, or if the company is repositioning from a standard industry to a unique industry to build value or competitive advantage. One of Saga Inc.'s flagship products was Straw Hat Pizza. When Ed started working with the company, its strategists defined its industry as pizza restaurants in a range of demographic markets. The only rivals Saga could see was other pizza places. This frame was strategically obsolete because the pizza industry was going through a transition. The cost to a family going out for pizza was rising; new rivals that were not in the pizza business, like Denny's, offered low-cost alternatives and higher values. Saga realized that Straw Hat Pizza was not in the pizza market but in the family diner market. Reframing the game it was in prompted Saga to adopt completely different measurements of the market, which eventually led to completely different strategic actions.

What matters particularly for competitive measurement is segmenting the market. Key benchmarks are market size, market growth and market share, which point to the company's attractiveness and position. Longitudinal market data show its relative position and attractiveness over time—a good indicator of its overall effectiveness and whether it is gaining or losing value.

With the segmentation in place, the team can name the competitors. In addition to the obvious rivals who offer the same type of product or service to the same customer segment or to adjacent segments, it helps to benchmark against leaders in the same general product space (for example, a bottled water company competes not only with other water companies, but with water utilities and perhaps with healthcare products) and even in substitutes (carmakers in Europe compete not only against each other, but also against government-owned train companies, and a substitute for commuting by car might be telecommuting from home). Say Company X produces merchandising software for second-tier retailers. In addition to its direct competitors selling the same product to first- and second-tier retailers, Company X is also a player in the retail software market (merchandising systems and other software for retailers) and in the general software market (all software for all customers). Even if companies in retail software and general software don't directly compete with its products today, Company X can gain valuable insights by comparing itself to leaders in those categories. And new entrants may compete with Company X in the future, for example web-based solutions or a low-cost software maker in India.

Financials can also serve as competitive metrics. Two good frameworks for this are a comparison of the company with its rivals in standard financials like the P&L, balance sheet and cash-flow; or the value-creation framework from Chapter 3 that compares sales growth, operating profit, capital turnover and cost of capital. For public companies market capitalization, enterprise value, shares outstanding, share price and trading volumes are other good categories. There may be more, depending on the dynamics of the industry, the transparency of the competition, and the money available to invest in competitive intelligence.

Program/Project Indicators. Remember: whatever you measure will run your life. And if the indicators are the wrong ones, they will measure your past, not your intended future, and will sabotage your prospects. As an example, take ending hunger again. Traditional indicators like GDP per capita or literacy rates or infant mortality are outcome indicators, not process indicators: They do not give rise to the actions that actually end hunger. What pulls for the right actions might be the percentage of children immunized, the ratio of girls getting a secondary education, or the amount of micro-lending for emerging businesses. Similarly, measuring share price or EBITDA alone may not give access to the strategic actions that build share price or EBITDA, which are the result, not the compelling pull for action you want in Strategy-In-Action.

Some actions defy counting, but still need to be monitored for achieving the strategic intent. Program and project measurement is particularly relevant when certain activities must be finished for the goal to be achieved, for example in R&D or product development or process improvement: activities that often run late or over budget and whose completion date is hard to forecast. One solution may be earned value systems, originally designed for very large, complex public-private partnerships such as space aviation, satellites, airplane platforms, or modernization programs that run for several years. When Ed worked at NASA's

AME Institute for Computation, he designed, built and readied one of the earliest earned value systems of record (he reported on this in his first master's thesis). The challenge was that the complexity of the mission control system of the Satellite Infrared Experiment (SIRE): 22 million lines of code. Ed and his team built a hierarchical program plan called a work breakdown structure (WBS), starting at the top with the program name and descending to major program functions, activities, tasks and so forth. A typical WBS on a large program is five to eight levels deep. Ed's team sized, budgeted and scheduled each level; the sum total became the planned program cost and schedule. The premise is straightforward. Only when activities are completed, and nothing less than 100 percent counts as complete, they become actual costs and schedules. All programs are planned with detailed time and cost schedules for each major and minor deliverable. To measure progress, planners take all elements that are 100 percent complete at a specific deadline ("actuals") and compare them regularly against their original forecasts for those milestones ("plan"). The benchmarks are a plan with timing and costing, a status update, a schedule and cost variance, and a cost to complete based on activities left. Instead of shooting in the dark with everyone's best guess, such a system allows for cutting through the complexity of measuring a multi-year project and gives you quantitative measures for making decisions.

In retail things are simpler. When Thomas worked with the European operation of the global energy company above on its strategic intent of "1 Euro more per customer," the retail team broke the intent down to program and project indicators, for example the monthly revenue of all gas station shops and their average monthly revenue outside of gas sales; the number of new shop customers; the percentage of "A" gas stations that served as "role models" to "B" and "C" gas stations of how great gas stations were run; and the percentage of independent gas station lessors who worked in partnership with corporate and had committed to the shop concept. The latter two benchmarks were themselves broken down into sub-indicators, for example the percentage of gas stations with their own baking shops that sold croissants and other fresh bakeries. Similarly, at the global bank, the team came up with these KPIs to pull for the right actions:

Performance	Metric
Productivity and efficiency	Cost per use case (point) Productivity factor
Leadership	360º feedback results Span of control, delegation degree
Retention top-talent	% of top performers retention % of meeting expectations (career path) % of internal mobility
Ownership	% accessibility of information Pulse check results
Behavioral compliance: Diversity, Leadership, Communication, Teamwork	MbO results (behavioral compliance mandatory)

Table 5.1: Performance and Metrics

The table nicely matches the metrics match where the team wants to go. At the risk of sounding like a broken record: unless each KPI lines up with the strategy and is directly tied to the strategic intent, the actions will likely backfire.

Case: Metrics for Performance in Bar-Coded Labels

Ed once ran a large label conversion subsidiary with a reputation as a pioneer in converting price tags to bar-coded labels and selling them to retailers and manufacturers. But lately the company had fallen upon hard times: it had problems getting its product to customers on time and was no longer profitable. Ed looked at the strategic, competitive, and financial indicators. When he compared the business with others in the industry, he found that its gross margins were very low. He dug deeper and saw that the costs of labor, the other direct costs, and the overhead were all more or less in line; the culprit was the material costs. Observing the manufacturing process, Ed noticed that most machine operators selected their customer jobs not on a first-in-first-out basis, or ganging (combining) jobs for efficiency, but first took the jobs they found easiest to run, regardless of the deadline promised to the customer. The manufacturing method was a three-step process, each step at a different workstation. The set-up of each job, at each station, generated significant waste, even when done efficiently. In the strategy session, Ed suggested that the operators run all jobs on a first-in first-out basis by customer commit date. Since jobs were staged in the equipment area before each workstation, this was easy to measure. Several times a day Ed walked the manufacturing floor and looked at staged jobs by workstation to measure the jobs. After a week, the operators had resolved the customer delivery issue.

The next attack was on the waste problem. The engineers designed a new piece of equipment that combined all three workstations into a single unit. This addressed about half the material cost overruns. Each workstation cost $1 million, and management had estimated that the payback period for this investment would be fifteen months. The actual break-even point ended up being four months.

Then Ed found that each operator's productivity could be improved by ganging jobs in a proper sequence instead of needing a new set-up for every job. As a metric, he and the strategy team chose total feet run by operator per machine shift. The data was available for each operator— management had collected the data for years but never used it—so the team posted the new statistics for all to see each operator's productivity.

The postings brought up a new problem. Individual operators were not keen to have everyone see their performance level, and concerned about both the accuracy and fairness of the benchmarks. So Ed and the managers met with the operators to address their qualms. They promised that they would not use the metrics for managing the operation until all operators were comfortable with the metrics. Further, they agreed to post all operators' results, but to list only each employee's number rather than his or her name. To make a long story short, the operators were willing to give it a try.

The results were phenomenal. Individual and overall performance improved significantly. Operators began to compete with each other and with themselves, going for personal bests. They came to see the indicator simply as a mirror of their performance, and their fear that the benchmarks might be used as a weapon against them faded. The process of design, acceptance, implementation, and integration of the metrics into the management control system took a while—five months—but the investment paid off: gross margins grew from 26 percent to 40 percent, on-time customer shipment jumped from 70 percent to 99 percent, and product quality improved from rejection rates of 7-10 percent to less than 1 percent. Other interventions were still needed in manufacturing and other areas, but this was a great first step. Everyone felt like a winner—operators, senior managers, and investors.

Getting these results took neither a sophisticated system nor a lot of metrics. But there were some key success factors: first, a shared understanding of the business; second, a competitive financial analysis; third, indicators that matched the intended results of key processes; fourth, a focus of everyone's attention on those indicators; and last but not least, the discipline to measure those indicators consistently.

Nobody is flawless. The strategy team made one key mistake: it failed to consult the operators on what benchmarks to use. That is why the managers met with the operators' pushback when they posted individual performance indicators. They had to step back, listen to the operators to understand and address their concerns, and then move forward again. Had they done so from the beginning, they would not have lost 30 days addressing the operators' concerns—easy to say with 20/20 hindsight. But Ed and the team learned their lesson. For a measurement system to gain acceptance, it pays to get buy-in from those being measured that the metrics are accurate, fair, and a match for their desired outputs. The system must grant all those whose productivity it measures access to the data, allowing them to use the data proactively and take corrective action quickly—themselves.

Ed and his team applied the lesson when they went into the customer service of the business, a 50-person operation of highly motivated people who loved what they did and were convinced they were doing a great job. When a customer called with a problem, the customer service representative would do whatever it took to fix the problem. This attitude earned them the customer's heartfelt thanks. What was less known was that many customer service practices were the very cause of the problems they had to fix.

Ed brought in some outside customer service experts to survey the customer base and evaluate the operation. But the contract required one difference: although managed by the consultants, the survey and evaluation had to be conducted by the internal staff. The staff eagerly participated in surveying their customers—and were devastated by what they heard. They thought their customers saw them as the best; they had no idea that they we doing less than an outstanding job. But since they themselves had done the survey and the evaluations, they could not argue with the results. Once motivated people recognize an issue and get help in coming up with solutions, it doesn't take long for them to own the way forward. This was the last step for the company in launching the growth mode that had eluded it for so long.

~

Boiling It Down

❑ Measurement *by itself* affects performance. Metrics can focus attention on specific areas. They can monitor operations, and help detect, resolve, and prevent problems.

❑ But measurement isn't free. The key questions to ask are: why measure, what, how, and how often? Over-measuring is costly; it can de-focus an operation and divert attention from your customers.

❑ Strategy-In-Action distinguishes five types of indicators: strategic, operational, financial, competitive, and program/project.

❑ Indicators can be either quantitative or qualitative. Some activities defy quantitative measurement but should still be monitored to realize the strategic intent.

❏ One tool for this is project management metrics, especially with complex activities for achieving a goal.

❏ Whatever you measure is bound to run your life, so make sure that your KPIs measure the achievement of the strategic intent, not simply what you used to measure in the past, which will produce more of the same—or backfire.

CHAPTER SIX

Filling the Gap: Thrusts and Synergies

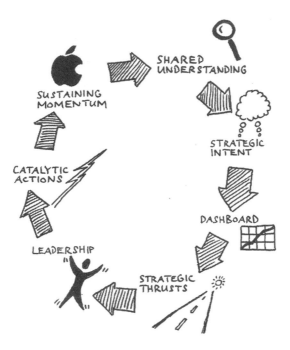

The man who insists on seeing
with perfect clearness before he decides,
never decides.
—Henri-Frédéric Amiel

In May 2010 Google announced a deal with Sony, Intel, and Swiss-based Logitech to offer Google TV, a seamless integration of television, the Internet, and its powerful capacity to organize information, designed to let any Internet users or viewers worldwide watch what and whenever they want. Google was not the only company to enter the television business. Since 2006, Apple had attempted to get into television with its Apple TV, a device that allows computer users to download, stream, and view high-definition television shows on demand via iTunes. Microsoft had been even earlier. In June 2001, CEO Steve Ballmer had been in Lisbon, basking in the glitter of assembled media cameras and in the glory of a small victory. TV Cabo had successfully tested Microsoft TV, the company's interactive television middleware. Six thousand miles away, in Silicon Valley, Microsoft TV's senior vice president Jon DeVaan was meeting with investors and technology executives, hoping to get the same in the United States: industry support, which had been elusive, for its middleware. Will Poole, vice president of Microsoft's Windows Digital Media division, gave Hollywood a hard sell of his own, calling on Viacom's chairman Jonathan Dolgen, a known Hollywood Luddite, to push Microsoft's media codec and rights-management software. Microsoft executives were conspicuously present at the Sundance Film Festival, the E3 gaming exposition, and all of the cable TV trade shows. "They are insidious," said Chris Lutz, the head of Mediachase, a broadband content developer in Los Angeles. "From my perspective, they are 100 percent on it."[79]

Why? Because Microsoft has a strategic thrust: to be seen by the entertainment industry not only as entertainment savvy, but as indispensable. Microsoft does not want to be a typical media company. It wants to supply the software that delivers all forms of entertainment to any playback device you could imagine. If successful, Microsoft will be *the* software platform used by executives to view digital dailies of movies they are funding, by directors to encode their demo reels, and by consumers to watch video on demand or listen to downloaded music.

While Microsoft is still known mostly for its Windows operating system and Office software suite, the company has been doggedly pursuing a major presence in the media business at least since 1994 when it bought special effects maker Softimage, at the time its second-largest acquisition ever. By 1996 it had invested over $6 billion annually in media-related enterprises, and that number grew only more when Microsoft started pushing its Windows Media Player, WebTV, and Xbox. Success was far from certain; in fact Microsoft had been involved in many skirmishes across the media landscape, from Disney and Sony to Nintendo and Linux, to name but a few rivals across the 21st-century media landscape. But according to Mr. DeVaan, "It's not important to win any particular battle. It is important only that you win the war."

That is the attitude. And you don't need to be Microsoft or Apple or Google to get obsessively committed to a strategic goal. Now that the strategy team has aligned on the benchmarks, the time has come to distill all the work done so far into a set of strategic thrusts that together achieve the strategic intent. Coming up with the right objectives is of course essential; they become the drivers of the strategy. To get at them, you have to revisit the key findings in the shared understanding (what's missing, what are the blockages, what are the opportunities?), your strategic vision and intent, and your strategic indicators, and lay them out in front of you. Their sum total, their synergies, and the gaps between the current situation and the desired future give the strategy its punch. Now it becomes operational and takes its first steps.

To define the strategic thrusts, the strategy team conducts a gap analysis—an assessment of how each element in the company supports (or fails to support) the strategic vision and intent. The gap analysis is where the rubber begins to hit the road. Depending on the shape of the company and the complexity of the vision, the strategy team may identify a handful or a large number of interrelated initiatives needed to achieve the strategic intent.

The depth of the analysis depends on what is needed to assess the company's strategic readiness; it varies from organization to organization. It may even vary within the same company, as critical elements go through in-depth analysis while others are analyzed the quick and dirty way—whatever depth is right for building an integrated roadmap that brings the strategy alive.

Each finding of the gap analysis goes into one of four categories: "winners" are existing activities necessary for the strategic vision and intent and currently effective; "problems" are existing activities necessary for the strategic intent but *not* effective; "talents" are activities that don't exist yet and that must be effective for the strategic intent; and finally, "losers" are existing activities *not* necessary for the strategic intent (see Table 6.1; the losers logically lie outside the table.)

Areas/Activities necessary for Strategic Vision & Intent	Existing	New
Effective/efficient	**Winners:** existing & effective	**Talents:** new & effective
Ineffective/inefficient	**Problems:** existing & ineffective	n/a

Table 6.1: Areas necessary for achieving strategic vision and intent

Obviously, the more activities are winners (existing and effective activities), the better. With the problems (existing and not effective), the gap process again defines how each area fits and what it would need to do to support the strategy. The team should give special attention to the changes needed to get the area up to par and fully supporting the strategy. For talents (new and seen as effective), the team positions each new area within the company, how it will contribute to achieving the company's goals, and what investments (time, money, people power) it will require. Finally, for losers (existing and no longer necessary), the team should find out what purpose, if any, these areas have served, what would happen if they remained, and the ramifications of trimming or dropping them. Losers suck up management attention and investment dollars that are better saved or placed elsewhere, so if possible the team should make decisive moves to terminate these activities. Of course such radical changes must be thought through to avoid unintended consequences or crises once the team decides to shrink or kill off an area.

The gap analysis yields a multi-layered map of the investment and/or implementation requirements of the strategy. Now team members—in the plenary or in task forces—can examine activities in each category to explore synergies. Synergy has become a buzzword; we are all fond of describing it as "one and one equals three." Synergy happens when two areas combine such that their sum is greater than their parts. Synergy can also mean two or more compatible, consistent, or mutually reinforcing areas. It is through synergies that companies create efficiency, leverage, scale, and momentum. In the 19th century Michael Faraday merged physics with chemistry and came up with electricity; all steps in a value chain work synergistically for optimal results; the generica of Sandoz synergize with the high-cost pharma products of Novartis to blanket a market.

Yet more often than not, top managers expect or promise synergies, for example from mergers, which never come to pass. The trick is to design the thrusts so that you get true convergence, like in music when every instrument is at its best and contributes to a powerful symphony because all musicians play from one score. But let's see first what a thrust is.

Strategic Thrusts

In the Strategy-In-Action framework, a strategic thrust is a key objective designed to provide what is missing for achieving the strategic intent. It is an initiative to pull the present to the desired future. The thrust is large-scale enough to serve as a building block of the strategic intent, yet short-term and achievable enough for each stakeholder to wrap his or her arms around and be energized. Each thrust stands on its own, yet works synergistically with the others and with the company as a whole.

When Thomas worked with Kazakhstan's prime minister, the cabinet, and then the Academy of Public Administration under the President, the question arose: If you want to improve economic output in the country, what would be the thrusts? Would you build railroads? Would you expand the Astana airport? Would you strive to make it easier for companies to locate in Kazakhstan? Would you invest in higher education? Kazakhstan is lucky to have vast resources and an almost limitless budget enabling the government to attack many thrusts at once; most organizations don't have that luxury and must prioritize, which means kissing lower-level priorities good-bye. So how do you choose the right thrusts?

Strategic thrusts are not a wish-list. They emanate from a rigorous analytical process that has made the strategy actionable. Solid and well thought-out thrusts are the foundation of successful execution. Here are six criteria: a strategic thrust has to be

- *Tied clearly to the strategic vision and strategic intent;*
- *Broad enough to achieve the desired result;*
- *Clear, concise, and compelling;*
- *Specific and without ambiguity about what is to be accomplished;*
- *Quantitatively measurable—usually in numbers, percentages or dollars; and*
- *An opening for action for stakeholders.*

Each thrust should meet all criteria. If one criterion is not met, the objective should be called into question and either reshaped or cancelled. Success (or failure) in execution depends largely on how well (or badly) defined and actionable the thrusts are. When the retail team of the first-tier energy company in the previous chapter set itself the strategic intent of 1 Euro more per customer, or a 16 percent increase, one ground rule was that the result had to come from the company's gas station shops—in other words, outside of revenue from petrol. Lessening the company's sole focus on gas sales made strategic sense in times of volatile oil prices and in anticipation of possibly scarce non-renewable commodities like oil. One key blockage the strategy team revealed was that the gas station owners were independent lessors loath to report to headquarters and reluctant to play the company's game. "For better or worse, we had to accept the independent gas station operators," one senior executive explained. "They don't make enough money—40,000 Euros per year on average—but they are not highly qualified so they don't have other opportunities. We can improve their education; and we can improve our external reps, each of whom is a liaison to 30 operators." One thrust the retail team set itself was to "Develop partnerships with all gas station operators and mobilize them with enthusiasm and passion for 16% plus." This thrust met all criteria above: it was in direct response to what was missing, it was clearly defined, and it worked. Within 18 months the gas station shops produced extra revenue of $75 million.

Often the question arises how many thrusts the team should take on. The answer is, as many as are needed to meet the strategic intent. Note that too many thrusts may cost you focus, disperse the team's energy in too many directions, and be more than the company can chew. THP distilled all the opportunities and demands for its work down to three major thrusts designed to provide exactly what's missing for the end of world hunger, nothing more, nothing less: Mobilize people at the grassroots level to build self-reliance; Empower women as key change agents; and Build partnerships with local governments. As a CEO, Ed has seen anywhere from six to twelve thrusts. In the management information systems department of a global financial services company, the strategy team set itself ten:

1. *Achieve current synergies: Achieve committed saves of 122m.*
2. *Lock in next year's synergies: Deliver signed-off plans to achieve committed saves of 166mm.*
3. *Deliver and operate stable and reliable platforms: Meet or beat performance benchmarks for production systems.*
4. *Talent management: Retain, develop and recruit the best talent in order to improve overall performance. In addition promote and reward our top performers.*
5. *Communication: Implement a communication framework for staff, clients and vendors that will increase awareness of and engagement with our activities.*
6. *Client delivery & alignment: Improve client delivery and organizational alignment.*

7. *Convergence: process, technology, organization: Process: establish single process architecture, in alignment with operating models. Technology: establish single converged technology infrastructure architecture. Organization: create integrated organization that has zero duplicated functions and works under a single operating model.*
8. *Data Center: Build and migrate to two new Data Center facilities. Gain approval and start build of an additional Data Center. In addition to the migration, take the opportunity to make a step-function change to the way in which we deliver infrastructure services and in the process: Standardize the environment at [X] component level or better. Increase utilization of the server footprint to 50%+. Consolidate the server footprint by 40%+.*
9. *Centers of Excellence: Leverage the Firm's deployment programs to create centers that enable innovation in process and technology.*
10. *Enable Service Oriented Infrastructure: Initial delivery of the technology and processes that will enable the rapid deployment of infrastructure capacity to precisely match the changing demands of our business.*

Besides what is needed for winning, a second consideration for the number of thrusts is the timeframe available: how long does the organization have to achieve its strategic intent, three years, five years?

A third item to think about is bandwidth: How many resources—financial and human—are available to implement the strategic thrusts? This is a moment where many strategies fail because strategists delude themselves about capacity. When considering investments and resources needed, the team should be mindful of opportunity costs: capacity requirements for the new strategy that would eat up existing day-to-day activities from the investment and resource pool. Many companies faced this dilemma during the Y2K scare leading up to the year 2000. In hindsight it seems slightly paranoid, but IT specialists and pundits worried that existing systems would stop working at the stroke of midnight because their embedded code was designed to only perform within a 20th-century time frame. At the turn of the century all systems would come to a standstill and all hell would break loose. So industry and government mobilized a massive effort to bring on line new systems with the proper embedded code just in time. But during implementation, they were dismayed to find they needed massive additional resources. In Ed's company, the six HR people were fully absorbed by their workload and could not be reassigned to Enterprise Resource Planning. This was true in every area of the company. ERP implementation forced many companies to stop all other strategic activities, focusing inward and lose touch with the marketplace. The only winners from the Y2K craze turned out to be ERP companies, IT consultants, and public accounting firms.

Hence a fourth thought is which day-to-day activities the team can bring into play for each strategic thrust. A high-tech company had developed image-guided dental surgery software, and then used that software also for training future dentists at universities. If current R&D activities can be redirected into new compelling products, this repurposing converts current operational expenses into strategic investments. The more the team can align current operations with the strategy, the better. But beware of unintended consequences: A company whose revenue depends on frequent new product introductions, say every six months, may have a revenue shortfall if significant R&D resources are redirected toward strategic activities with development cycles longer than six months.

Finally, sequencing matters. To meet one objective, a company might need to first meet another. If you bring a new product to market, you have to build a new distribution system to drive the product into the marketplace. Without smart timing, you might run up massive sunk costs for investments that sit idle and get obsolete while they wait way too long for prerequisite milestones to be met. Both the CEO and the strategy team should keep in mind the big picture of the overall project and implement the sequence in the required order.

One of the stakeholder groups you must watch closely in that sequence is the board of directors. Boards can throw a wrench into long and complex strategy implementations, since they typically like to see results and sit far enough from the business that they may forget the details or not fully grasp the nuances. This does not mean you have bad board members, but one that needs frequent communication on your strategic process. We have addressed this need with a short slide deck at the beginning of each board meeting, bringing back the strategy, key initiatives and status, followed by a brief discussion. This half-hour helps the CEO manage alignment between the board and the executive team. To paraphrase Jack Welch: communicate, communicate, and communicate. We cannot say this enough. It is the only way you can check your assumptions and blind spots, and make sure nothing is lost in translation.

After considering the number of thrusts, the investment and resource capacity, the repurposing of existing activities, and the timing, the team should be filled with confidence that the strategic thrusts will converge to achieve the strategic intent. Sorry, but if that confidence is not palpable or lacking altogether, the strategy team has to revisit the strategic vision and strategic intent, the indicators and the gap analysis until it has the right mix.

Derailers of Strategic Thrusts

If the Strategy-In-Action process has been facilitated properly, each stakeholder on the strategy team is fully invested. The team members have stepped out of their day-to-day routines, they are thinking strategically, and perhaps they are even venturing beyond group-think or ready-made conclusions. Most important, team members are excited and energized from seeing the whole puzzle come together.

If on the other hand the strategic thrusts don't quite converge synergistically, it may be a good idea to reassess the group dynamics. The facilitator has to be aware that Strategy-In-Action is a unique experience for the strategy team; it can shatter cherished beliefs; it can bring hidden discord out in the open and set people against each other; it can be tedious or downright exhausting. For some participants the shared understanding has left open too many issues, conclusions are not robust enough, or other team members are not pulling their weight. Sometimes a time-out is necessary. When Ed experienced this blockage, he and the team took stock of all the unresolved items, assigned task forces to get the information, suspended the process and set a time for a re-launch. Once the task forces had gathered the knowledge needed, the group came back together 30 days later and moved forward.

Other participants lose confidence in the feasibility of the strategic intent. To address this issue, the team has to revisit and re-examine the strategic vision, and either embrace it or change it to one they can wrap their arms around.

Yet other strategy team members feel overwhelmed with details. If so, it is little use to shove the process down their throats. There is always room for filling in more details in a second round.

Rude comments or lack of courtesy can shut people down and poison the atmosphere. One individual or faction can dominate the whole group. Naysayers can be disruptive and derail the process. Such issues must be dealt with immediately, proactively, and firmly, with open communication and straight talk that put the issues on the table to they can be tackled.

Lastly, attempts by the process leader to hijack the discussion or push through a pre-cooked agenda are the death knell of Strategy-In-Action, whose strength lies in giving voice to all views and in aligning on all key decisions. To maximize the number of participants with voice, the facilitator can break the plenary into subgroups. Breakouts can be a good way to speed up the work; they mix things up so participants stay fresh and alert; they allow people to dig deeper into a specific issue; and they spread opportunities for leadership. When each breakout group presents its findings and discusses them with the plenary, each team has to lead. Which brings us to the next phase of Strategy-In-Action: putting in place the leaders who will execute the strategy.

$\sim$

Boiling It Down

❑ Strategic thrusts are major objectives designed to provide what 's missing, break through key blockages, and/or seize opportunities for achieving the strategic intent. They are typically five to seven drivers that pull the present to the future. They are broad enough to accomplish the strategic intent, yet short-term enough for each participant to wrap his or her arms around and be energized.

❑ A strategic thrust must be: tied clearly to the strategic vision and intent; concise and compelling; without ambiguity about what is to be accomplished; quantitatively measurable; and articulated in compelling language to mobilize key stakeholders.

❑ To align on the thrusts, the strategy team conducts a gap analysis in which it revisits the work done so far: the shared understanding, the strategic vision and intent, and the metrics. The key categories of the gap analysis are winners (current areas necessary for the strategic intent and currently effective); problems (current and necessary but not effective); talents (new areas whose effectiveness will be necessary); and losers (current areas not necessary).

CHAPTER SEVEN

Leadership, Power, Culture

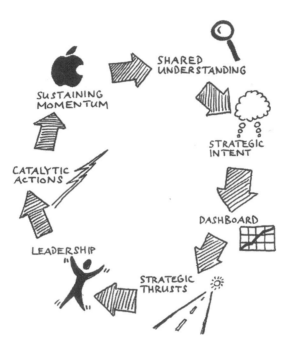

The greatest need for leadership is in the dark...
It is when the system is changing so rapidly...
that old prescriptions and old wisdoms can only lead to catastrophe
and leadership is necessary to call people to the very strangeness
of the new world being born.
—Kenneth Boulding

The year 2008 marked the celebration of General Motors' 100th anniversary. Somewhat ironically, it also marked the first year since the 1930s that G.M. could no longer call itself the world's largest automaker. That year, Toyota sold 620,000 more cars than G.M.

The celebration did not last. Barely a year later, the company and its stock were hammered by reports that thousands of Toyotas and Lexus had crashed due to a terrible combination of sudden, automatic accelerations and unresponsive brakes. But it turned out, according to testing by the National Highway Trafic Safety Administration, the accidents were probably due to thousands of human errors. Was Toyota the victim of bad drivers, greedy lawyers, and U.S. politicians eager to champion U.S. carmakers, or did it hide something? Was the company innocent until proven guilty, or guilty until proven innocent?

Reports showed that Toyota executive Katsuhiko Koganei had sent an email to his U.S. colleagues in January 2010, urging them to "not mention about the mechanical failures." At the time, Toyota spokesman Irv Miller shot back: "We are not protecting our customers by keeping this quiet... The time to hide on this one is over. We need to come clean." These internal memos gave a strong impression that the carmaker was hiding problems with its accelerators. And blaming 3,000 drivers was "totally ludicrous," said former NHTSA chief Joan Claybrook at consumer advocate Public Citizen. "They should be looking at the electronics in their cars and everyone knows it."[80]

Both U.S. federal investigators and Toyota executives countered that "virtually all" Toyota crashes were caused by driver error. According to them, many Toyota drivers had put their foot on the gas instead of the brakes. Toyota engineers did their own testing of 2,000 wrecked cars, and came to the same conclusion: "virtually all" crashes were due to drivers who hit the gas instead of the brakes. But as the company's president Akio Toyoda said, blaming customers was not part of the company's PR strategy.

Whether or not the scandal was just the latest result of sensation-hungry media that blew the story out of proportion, this much is clear: even before the controversy, Toyota was not known as a very creative company.

Case: The Toyota Way

Toyota was great at imitation, not invention. Drivers liked, but did not love, their Toyotas. *Fortune*, usually an effusive fan of the company, called it "stodgy and bureaucratic."[81] But what Toyota has done, perhaps better than any other manufacturing company, is to build a cohesive culture, and to live that culture in the action; in short, turning principle into practice. The principles of its Toyota Production System are simple, even obvious: kill waste; fix problems the moment they come up; get auto parts the moment workers need them. Toyota's philosophy is not even new: Taiichi Ohno, the engineer and main architect of the Toyota Production System during the resource-poor years after World War II, cited Henry Ford and American supermarkets as his inspirations.

So what's the difference? One answer is that we tend to think of innovation as *what* is made. What Toyota reinvented was *how* things are made so it could build cars faster and with less labor than American companies. It invented things like the *andon* cord, which any worker can pull to stop the assembly line if he or she notices a problem, or *kanban*, a card system that allows workers to signal when new parts are needed. This reorganized factory floors and workspaces for a freer and easier flow of parts and products.

The Toyota Production System has been widely copied, the company freely opens its plants for tours, and it even embarked on a joint venture with GM designed, at least in part, to help GM improve its own production system. Over the years, more than 3,000 books and articles have analyzed how the company works, and things like *andon* systems are now common sights on factory floors. Many of Toyota's doctrines have changed how other auto makers operate and have made the entire industry far more productive than it used to be. Yet despite the recent uproar around its faulty brakes, Toyota has kept the edge. How does it stay ahead of the pack?

Another answer lies in another facet of Toyota's culture called *kaizen*—continuous improvement. Instead of trying to make giant leaps, Toyota moves in continuous baby-steps. This also means that it does not delegate innovation to the R&D department, but sees it as a daily task for which all—managers and workers alike—take responsibility. Matthew E. May, the author of a book about Toyota, writes that the company implements a million new ideas a year, and most of them come from ordinary workers.[82] (Japanese companies get a hundred times as many suggestions from their workers as U.S. companies do.) The ideas can be tiny—making parts on a shelf easier to reach, say—and not all of them work. In 2006, Toyota ran into not just one but a series of quality problems. But every day, Toyota learns a bit more, and does things a little better, than it did the day before.[83] And it does so by empowering its people to be change agents. In a small way, everyone becomes a leader.

Co-Leaders at All Levels

Strategy stands or falls with the quality of the leadership executing it. The equation is simple: No leadership, no execution. Even the best strategy remains wishful thinking unless the company has leaders with the right competencies at the right levels. True, the CEO is ultimately responsible for strategy formulation and execution; this responsibility cannot be delegated; the burden comes with the job. But in a world of business that spins ahead at a dizzying pace, with unforeseen demands from customers and sudden attacks from competitors who were not even on the scene until last week (or so it seems), who should be in command of the firm as it faces these challenges—the supreme solitary leader who makes flash decisions and never second-guesses himself? Maybe not. We have already seen that these days reality is far too complex for lone rangers. What's called for are collaborative leaders—co-leaders—who know that no matter how brilliant or experienced they are, they face too many variables to master alone. Co-leaders reach broadly and deeply into the organization for input on decisions and partnership in execution. "A leader these days has to be facilitative," says Rod Stephens, vice president of sales operations for office furniture manufacturer Herman Miller. "Not the one who gives all the answers himself, but gathers answers among the collective intelligence around him." Stephens points out that advanced communications technology makes it possible to collect the thinking of all employees and thereby evaluate strategies before executing them. "You can make use of the organization's entire know-how," he says, "not merely that of the five or six people on top."[84] According to McKinsey, a company's leadership reaches well beyond a few good men and women at the top, and typically includes the three to five percent of employees who can deliver breakthroughs in performance.[85] Strategy execution is a long-term and resource-intensive commitment. It needs consistent pull at multiple management layers, the constant question, "Who will get this done?" and the willingness to tell—and hear—the truth, or the organization will revert back to the status quo as soon as the CEO and/or the strategy team move on to the next agenda item.

But many CEOs get little or no straight talk from their insular circle of advisors; even if a CEO's senior people dare speak unvarnished truth to power, and even if they don't get penalized, singled out or excommunicated for calling a spade a spade, the CEO may not care to listen and instead merely reconfirms his or her already-existing bias.

And those CEOs or chief strategists who are open to collaborative leadership face another problem: getting leaders with the right stuff to implement the strategy. In complex environments with highly mobile executives, finding the truly valuable players has become harder. Only three percent of companies surveyed by Corporate University Xchange felt they are able to find the leadership talent they need. The other 97 percent of surveyed organizations said they are concerned about their current leadership bench strength or their ability to develop the leadership talent they need to meet their growth objectives. (81 percent said they are "significantly concerned.")[86] "In the past it was relatively easy to tell who in marketing developed the best product plans, or who in sales had the best results," said Brian Schipper, senior vice president of human resources at Cisco Systems. The search for collaborative leaders who know how to ask for assists across the organization gives the tech company new headaches as it looks for implementation talent. "It is now a lot more subtle, because you are looking for individuals who are getting results not only in their own areas of expertise but working collaboratively with others in other functions."[87]

To develop that bench strength, top managers need humility (knowing they don't know everything and letting others grow and stand out) and the guts to involve colleagues in their decisions. The late football coach Bill Walsh put it this way: "Successful coaches realize that winning teams are not run by single individuals who dominate the scene and reduce the rest of the group to marionettes." While Walsh spoke about coaches; he could have just as well meant CEOs.

Some are not afraid to reach out to voices that might disagree with them. When Thomas worked with the energy company we know from previous chapters, the managing director who sponsored the project took care to involve stakeholders from across the organization: senior managers in corporate headquarters, leaders in the field, liaisons with the gas station owners, young and hungry managers as well as more seasoned ones. This cross-functional and cross-generational mix yielded a richer tapestry of perspectives for thinking the strategy through from all vantage points. Of course the deliberations took longer than with unilateral decision-making, and the managing director was at times given to impatience and tempted to go back to a top-down style. But as we saw in the previous chapter, the investment paid off. It's hard to argue with $75 million in additional top-line growth.

Bringing In More Stakeholders

For optimal execution, Strategy-In-Action must expand beyond the small strategy group that has driven formulation. The question is when and how the company gets involved. Typically, that time comes after the strategy team has aligned on the strategic thrusts, but before it crafts detailed execution plans. There are exceptions; sometimes a broader group brings the necessary domain expertise to check a key thrust—for example a new technology or a product roadmap—and to grasp the implications of each option even before alignment on that objective.

The CEO should call on three groups; each is integral to the process. Some participants belong to more than one group; the CEO often belongs to all three. The **sponsors** support the strategy process and grant authority to the strategy team. In a public company, the board of directors is responsible for ensuring that a strategy is in place, resourced properly, and executed effectively. The CEO is part of the sponsor group, plus he or she is responsible for articulating and executing a winning strategy. The **strategy team** works with the CEO on strategy formulation and is co-accountable for execution, with each member responsible for one or more specific components. Individual **change agents** are the implementers, the army of change within the company. They work at various levels across the company; some are managers, others key employees, company boosters, opinion leaders, and role models who can demonstrate new and better ways to work. What motivates them is the professionalism of doing the right thing, being the best they can be, and making the company better. It is on their backs that strategy implementation falls.

The CEO and/or facilitator sets up a series of small group sessions, every semester or annually, announced or informal, to touch employees and get their views. The meetings are small, limited to ten or twelve employees. Most are by business function: product development, marketing, sales, accounting, and so forth; some mix functions, for example when a new product affects QA, marketing, and customer service. The rules are that any topic can be discussed; whatever is said in the meeting is confidential and will not leave the room. To combine the outputs with those of other groups, the facilitator takes notes or assigns someone else to do so. One way to foster honesty and straight talk is to make meetings peer-to-peer instead of employees with supervisors.

Some meetings cover specific topics the facilitator sees as crucial to strategy implementation, others are more generic. Either way, five questions for the agenda are, What do we do well? What could we improve? Why do people buy our product or services? What do you like about the company? And, If you where the boss, what three things would you change?

The added value of these meetings is that the CEO checks the shared understanding, vision, metrics and strategic thrusts with the front-line people who are closest to the customer or the job at hand. It is a win-win for everyone and starts the company down the path of aligned execution. Management benefits since the CEO can credibly represent the views of the employee base and bear them in mind as fully as those of other stakeholders. Employees benefit since they get voice and feed their ideas directly into the strategy. Above all, the strategy benefits: In the companies where we applied Strategy-In-Action, employee meetings typically led to 80 percent of the strategic inputs.

To bring the board, management and other key contributors (alliances or suppliers, investors or customers) into the process, the facilitator typically holds one or more two-day sessions. If there is more than one, management and key contributors come first and lead up to a board session. A member of the strategy team presents the findings for each Strategy-In-Action phase. After each step, participants might split into breakout groups facilitated by strategy team members. The aim of such breakouts is to broaden participation, seek creative inputs, strengthen the strategy, find alternative perspectives and pathways, and most importantly, prepare people for individual stretch assignments that match the overall strategy. To get strong buy-in, strategy team members must be open to other stakeholders challenging their straw man.

After each breakout session, the plenary reconvenes to validate and commit to the proposed straw man or to revise a strategy component until there is an acceptable solution. The two-day session results in a strategy that all key stakeholders can align on, commit to, and act on. If the board meets on its own, the process is similar. Strategy team members and board members join teams based upon strengths and weaknesses of various individuals, existing relationships and future relationships that could be relevant to implementation. For example, one key relationship is between the CFO and the board member that chairs the audit committee. If any holes remain, the strategy team gathers once more, vets the final strategy, and reconciles any gaps between the board's strategy and management's strategy.

To repeat once again: employees get excited when they see that senior management listened to them, when they recognize their ideas in the strategy, ideas for issues that may have long frustrated them if the company failed to address problems or pursue opportunities. Seeing these elements now on the table as part of the new strategy will give the workforce new energy—180 degrees different from when you roll out a pre-cooked top-down strategy. In each session, participants can challenge elements and come up with alternatives, which are carefully reviewed and adopted, rejected or refined. The result is priceless: strategic alignment across the organization, no mean feat in today's fast-moving business environment. We cannot think of a company or organization that won't benefit from this approach. The process gives all company levels and functions a chance to play in strategy design and direction, and to set the stage for individuals to accept accountability for making it happen.

On Accountability

This brings us to a key word: accountability. Strategy implementation starts and ends with it. Being accountable is akin to being pregnant: you are either 100 percent accountable or you are not. There is no such thing as 50 percent or 90 percent accountability. You are fully accountable, and your results will show that, or you are merely helping out, and the results will show *that*. Life is an implacable, incorruptible mirror of accountability and the lack thereof. As the word says, when you are accountable, you can be counted on to do whatever it takes to produce the result.

For company leaders at all levels to take 100 percent accountability, the strategy team must make the expectations crystal clear. Two quick stories to illustrate what happens when accountability is absent and when it's present. When Random House, then the world's largest trade publisher, shocked the book world in late 2001 by hiring Phyllis Grann, the former CEO of Penguin Putnam, as vice chairman, it seemed like a major coup. The two companies were sworn archrivals. Grann, a small woman even in heels, with a youthful face that made her look younger than her age, was the first woman CEO in the world of publishing. Starting out as a secretary to the publisher Nelson Doubleday, she had risen to the top job with her nose for page-turning novels and her knack for high-voltage marketing, and had turned Penguin Putnam into a virtual factory for turning out blockbusters. Hiring Grann, Random House chairman Peter Olson said at the time, was like persuading "Michael Jordan to come back and play on any team in any position."[88] But Olson made one big mistake: He failed to make Grann's exact role clear in advance. In a memo introducing her new "corporate advisory position" as vice chairman, he had written:

> Although Phyllis will have no specific day-to-day publishing or editorial responsibilities, our adult and children's publishers worldwide will be welcome to draw upon her experience in planning a specific book or publishing program. She will be a wonderful collaborator, especially when working with our publishers on projects of mutual interest. The publishers, as always, will make the final decision about whether a project is a good editorial and financial fit for them."[89]

While such effusive praise feels good, it does not clarify accountability. Grann was accountable for no results and to nobody. The consequences of her unclear brief came soon enough. People close to her reported she grew bored and frustrated with the lack of definition in her role. Her associates said she joked that for years she gave Olson her advice and he never used it; now she got paid for it too. By July 2002, Grann, one of the most commercially successful publishers in recent history, was already history herself, having left her new job.

In sharp contrast to this story stands THP, one of the most skillful organizations at marshaling people's accountability, where some one hundred staff members worldwide coordinate over 50,000 local volunteer leaders worldwide. This makes for huge leverage and return on investment: one dollar stretches far with such minimal overhead. Here are the organization's "basic principles of being on staff"[90] that make crystal-clear what the job is. These operating principles help build a culture of accountability.

Basic Principles of Being on Staff

Vision: To always see a future that one stands for, that gives meaning and purpose to one's actions.

Commitment: To work out of a deep personal commitment to the end of hunger and to the unique mission, mandate and focus of THP in achieving that goal.

Privilege: To possess the spirit of contribution and service, with a deep appreciation for the privilege it is to do the work of THP.

Responsibility: To be personally and individually responsible for the whole Hunger Project. When someone meets one of us, they are meeting someone who represents and stands committed to the entire organization.

Teamwork: To work as one, unified team, as one strategic organization with one strategic intent and one set of objectives.

Empowerment: To empower each other; to be committed to each other's success.

Alignment: To be able to create a place to stand together to see what's wanted and needed, and from there to co-create our work out of alignment, rather than as a compromise among differing points of view.

Flexibility: As members of a strategic organization, to be obsessed with achieving our mission, and totally unattached to any particular pathway to achieving it.

Communication: To be committed to complete and honest communication that is clear, straightforward and timely.

Integrity: To be committed to the power of the truth, to our own integrity and to the total integrity of THP.

Breakthroughs: To possess the courage and determination to achieve breakthroughs rather than mere incremental advances. To not sell out to circumstances, and to achieve "unreasonable" results on a regular basis.

Breakdowns: To declare breakdowns when they occur—to have the courage, responsibility and discipline of always delivering the "bad news first."

Professionalism/Complete staff work: To be committed to doing complete staff work—work characterized by excellence, impeccability and professionalism.

Intention: To have clear intentions, and stay true to our purpose line in our work.

Methodology: To utilize and master one, unified "THP" style and technology of producing results, one culture, one spirit of excellence and momentum of accomplishment.

Workability: To create a clean and empowering physical environment for our work—one that pulls for clarity and productivity. To not tolerate unworkability.

Self-reliance: To be self-reliant. To be responsible for being informed and getting what we need to do our jobs.

The CEO's Job: One Size Does *Not* Fit All

What about the expectations of the CEO? What is his or her job in leading Strategy-In-Action? The CEO may have to be a different type of leader at different times—in other words, vary his or her leadership style and methods depending on the work at hand, the company culture, and what's needed for best results. Leadership needs, and hence leadership style, change as the company moves from strategy design to execution. In the execution phase, the CEO moves from a participatory style to a directive style, including accountability, authority, and tools; well defined and agreed-upon milestones and deliverables; and systematic monitoring. Certainly there are still participative activities in strategy, policy or problem solving; but the keys to implementation are discipline, correction, and performance coaching. The roles, responsibilities, and expectations should be clear-cut; the ground rules should be written, understood, and honored. If the CEO openly discusses leadership styles with the staff, this will create the "no surprise" environment essential to building trust.

The secret to long-term success, said consultant David Nadler at a Wharton conference several years ago, is to think of a CEO's tenure as a performance with a series of distinct acts. "Each act requires the CEO to lead, think and behave in fundamentally different ways."[91] Take Carly Fiorina and her five-and-a-half year tenure as the former CEO of Hewlett-Packard. Despite her controversial acquisition of Compaq, she made the right moves, at least early on. "In act one, she was required to create a transformation at HP, develop a new strategy, break the static elements and reshape the business through the acquisition," Nadler said. "Given that [her successor] Mark Hurd has kept the same fundamental strategy, she probably did the right things." Fiorina's problems came when act one ended and act two began— execution. A "hunkering down," not a CEO in the limelight, was needed to get the job done. "Instead, she continued on the same approach, and the leadership model that had been successful in act one killed her in act two."

The counter-example to Fiorina is E. Stanley O'Neal, who took the helm at Merrill Lynch just three months after 9/11 literally blew the company out of its global headquarters in lower Manhattan. The company's woes ran deeper, though, reflected in a plunging stock price and rumors of a takeover. O'Neal approached these challenges with a management style Nadler described as "demanding, almost brutal at times." He focused relentlessly on control, discipline, and cost. "His feeling was, 'I have to save the company. If I don't do this, we'll be finished and thousands of jobs will be gone.'"

The company began to recover, and by the fall of 2003 O'Neal did something different: He changed his entire executive team, focused on growth, and rethought his own leadership style. By 2007, with Merrill's stock trading at nearly three times what it had in 2001, O'Neal began building up the next generation of leaders. He created two co-presidents who operated alongside him as co-CEOs. He began seeing his job mostly as "being a mentor, coach and supporter." The bottom line: it's situational leadership. The CEO must think hard about what each phase of Strategy-In-Action needs from top management, and then be the leader the situation demands.

Culture Eats Strategy for Breakfast

One key job of the CEO is setting the culture that is a match for the desired future. This is not an afterthought. Louis Gerstner, widely credited with turning around IBM before retiring as chairman and CEO in 2002, once said about his strategy: "Fixing the culture is the most critical—and most difficult—part of a corporate transformation."[92] Gerstner knew that culture can be the most insidious enemy of strategic change—that culture eats strategy for breakfast any day. And you cannot just exchange the people—culture is sticky. That's why organizational change is so difficult. It's a vicious cycle: behaviors, and at their source attitudes and mindsets, are deeply embedded and reinforced every day. If there is a silo mentality, for example, then most employees, most of the time, will take actions matching that silo mindset, from ingratiating themselves with their bosses to building personal fiefdoms to keeping vital intelligence from their colleagues in other departments. One company might even boast multiple cultures. In one global corporation that resulted from several cross-border mergers, the private bankers were mostly Europeans in Zurich—more risk-averse, reserved, frugal and tight-fisted, and hierarchical—while the investment bankers were mostly Americans in New York City—more risk-friendly, testosterone-driven, free-wheeling, and participatory. This led to serial misunderstandings and culture clashes.

A key tenet of Strategy-In-Action is that the organizational culture must match the strategy. How do you decode the current culture, and how do you align it with your vision? A good start is to match the company's declared and codified values against real day-to-day behaviors. Can you guess which company came up with these core values?

Core Values

"RESPECT: We treat others as we would like to be treated ourselves. We do not tolerate abusive or disrespectful treatment. Ruthlessness, callousness, and arrogance don't belong here.

"INTEGRITY: We work with customers and prospects openly, honestly and sincerely. When we say we will do something, we will do it; when we say we cannot or will not do something, we won't do it.

"COMMUNICATION: We have an obligation to communicate. Here, we take the time to talk with one another... and to listen. We believe that information is meant to move and that information moves people.

"EXCELLENCE: We are satisfied with nothing less than the very best in everything we do. We will continue to raise the bar for everyone. The great fun here will be for all of us to discover just how good we can really be."

These beautiful values are from a company lauded throughout the 1990s as exemplary by the likes of *Fortune* magazine and *The New York Times*. They are from the company's 1998 annual report. The company is now defunct. You probably guessed right: it was Enron. The values made zero difference, since the fish stank from the head—Enron's senior managers didn't bother to live by them. Take just the one about communication. When Sherrone Watkins took her "obligation to communicate" seriously enough to come to Jeffrey Skilling, the CEO did not heed the value "and to listen." The gulf between word and deed proved too wide.

Are people living the company's values in their day-to-day actions, or are they merely giving lip-service? Do managers and employees communicate openly, or gossip excessively? (For example, Microsoft created a "clear escalation" rule that explicitly forbids talking about a problem with someone who cannot do something about it.) Do they take responsibility, or do they pass the buck? Do they take risks and show entrepreneurial spirit, or do they wait for someone else to stick his or her neck out? Do they say "I" or "we" (Johnson & Johnson discourages the use of the selfish "I" in communications)? Xerox can tell a story about the power of values. One of the great success stories in American corporate history, the pioneer of photocopiers began to falter in the 1990s as high costs translated into uncompetitive prices, and by 2001, Xerox saw its stock price plunging 92 percent in under two years, decreasing cash, a worsening market position, and to top it off an SEC investigation. Some pundits questioned whether Xerox would survive as an independent company. Anne Mulcahy, who did not even make the initial list of CEO candidates, caught the attention of the board with her passion and dedication for the company and its culture. When Mulcahy became CEO in 2001 (and chairman in 2002), after working her entire career deep inside the corporation, she refused to destroy the company in order to save it. ("I am the culture," she said. "If I can't figure out how to bring the culture with me, I'm the wrong person for the job.") Churchillian in her belief that Xerox people could prevail against all odds, she refused to capitulate, sell out, or see defeat as inevitable. From losses of more than $300 million in 2000 to 2001, she righted the company to more than $1 billion in 2007 profits.[93] Her successor Ursula Burns, at Xerox since 1980 when she had joined as a mechanical engineering summer intern, kept on with the same core values.

With the right culture, people can overcome huge odds. In 1965 Nucor Corp., then less than a hundredth the size of the market leader Bethlehem Steel, was on the verge of bankruptcy. Faced with a hodgepodge of unrelated businesses and deteriorating debt ratios, the board made a desperate move: it turned the company over to a division manager named Ken Iverson, just 39 at the time. "Here, you're too young to know any better," the board seemed to say. "You take it!" Iverson had run Nucor's only successful division, where he'd built a weird culture of crazed productivity making steel joists. After jettisoning the worst divisions, he began to build, and build, and build. He and his team backward-integrated into making raw steel, creating a mini-mill, and discovered that Iverson's culture could be harnessed to produce the lowest-cost steel in America. Step by step, year by year, Iverson's team added capacity, eventually breaking onto the Fortune 500 at No. 481 in 1980. In a brutally competitive steel industry, Nucor kept a solid No. 151 ranking on the Fortune 500, with 41 years of consecutive profitability. As a testament to the durability of Nucor's culture, and its respect for its people, the annual report continues a long-held tradition of naming every Nucor employee, more than 18,000 individuals.[94]

Like Iverson, at times you have to go against the prevailing culture that has all the votes. When Thomas held a leadership workshop for the government cabinet of Kazakhstan, he asked the prime minister right at the outset, "Do you realize that most of the people in this room don't tell you the truth?" The heads of several cabinet ministers jerked up in disbelief at the open challenge to what was evidently a taboo. It was a gamble. Thomas had asked the question on purpose: he wanted to expose a golden calf in the room. The prime minister only cocked his head slightly and said nothing. Silence. Thomas pressed on: "Do you realize that they tell you only what *they think* you want to hear?" After what seemed like a very long silence, the prime minister broke into a broad smile and said, "Ah!" The entire cabinet said "Ah!" and chuckled with him. It is the same with many CEOs: They cannot count on their top managers to tell them the naked truth. Thomas' questions were designed to wake the participants up to an unwritten rule of behavior that nobody questioned anymore. That is culture: a set of assumptions and behaviors that are challenged rarely if ever, typically implicit rather than explicit, and seldom even conscious. If asked about them, people would shrug and say, "It's simply the way we do things around here."

Culture is a result of history. The CEO of one Swiss telecom that worked with Strategy-In-Action found that the company originally specialized in call centers and had been, from its founding in 1984 through 1998, a virtually exclusive supplier to the Swiss PTT (Post, Telephone, Telegraph), a national agency. This past condition had made for a deeply entrenched culture with the following symptoms: an employee mentality of big government bureaucracy (a lack of self-reliance, weak customer service, weak responsibility or initiative, weak cost discipline and a palpable lethargy in certain departments); a "survival syndrome" in certain managers who had survived two takeovers by a larger company, and fears of yet another merger; and a lack of confidence among employees in the viability of the company (management had tried change before and it hadn't worked). But there were also many positive aspects of the company's culture, for example its deep domain expertise; a significant client base; its maintenance and supplier contracts already in place; and esteem by the market.

One big irony of culture change is that the very same people who have the most power to cause change—the C-level managers at headquarters—are the people who have the strongest incentive to keep the status quo in place. It's a logical chain: The more you are invested in the way things are now, the more you have to lose from change, and the more you want to avoid change. The bottom line: make sure you define the culture that is congruent not with the past gave you but with the future you want.

Rigging the Incentives

One way to get the desired culture is of course to rig the incentives that will pull for the right being and actions. Incentive systems can take many forms. You have to stand in the shoes of your people and ask yourself, what would knock their socks off? To lure Brett Shanaman from an old-economy company, WetFeet.com agreed to sponsor his hobby: racecar driving. Soon after Kevin Vela had joined iThought.com, he got the key to a company car for the weekend, just for completing a project ahead of schedule. The "car" was a Hummer. LoweringBills.com rewarded workers not only with stock options, but also by paying their recurring bills for one month and treating them to skydiving trips. But "Gimmicks don't make good people stay," said Dimitri Boytan, a co-founder and later CEO of Hotjobs.com. "Growth and opportunities are what makes the environment work."[95] Like our colleague Daniel Pink, we argue that incentives work only for simple repetitive actions and not for complex ones, and that people need a future and a challenging and fulfilling job. Strategy-In-Action is designed to meet those needs. The problem is that even if you don't have any formal incentives, some will be there by default (among them comfort, peer pressure, saving face, or being popular); unless you choose them deliberately, you will likely get unintended consequences.

Stakeholders translate the strategic intent and thrusts into personal MBOs and deliverables, and negotiate measurements, the backbone of the performance management system. Their short-term incentives might fall within a twelve-month period and might include profit sharing, performance bonuses, stock awards, and spot bonuses. Long-term incentives last usually one to five years and might feature stock options, restricted stock, and special bonuses. To find and keep good people, wages and benefits, short-term and long-term incentives must be competitive. The Strategy-In-Action process assumes that a competitive compensation system is in place; if not, one of the strategic thrusts should address that.

The mismatch comes when designers have not thought through all the consequences of an incentive system. One frequent pitfall is that salespeople may maximize earnings by taking the company into unplanned and risky shenanigans. Many a company has seen its sales growth scuttled or its strategic focus evaporate due to inadvertent results from its sales incentives. The irony is that this often occurs because the sales force is doing *exactly* what the incentives compelled them to do. The compensation system should be designed to track the behaviors and results the company wants to reward, and to calculate the salesperson's commissions. Good salespeople study the system thoroughly to understand how they can achieve the highest payout. We tend to forget a simple rule: people tend to do exactly what they are enticed to do. It is incumbent on the company to ensure that the actions and results it fosters with its incentives are in fact what it *wants* to achieve; mismatches are all too common. If asset managers are compensated not based on maximizing their clients' wealth, but with bonuses from their bank based on maximizing the bank's profits, it eventually leads to suboptimal results, if not a financial crisis.

Now that the shared understanding, strategic intent, indicators of success, thrusts and leadership/culture are aligned upon, the strategy is complete and can move into execution. The next phase is to design, launch and deliver short-term catalytic projects that pull the future to the present.

~

Boiling It Down

❑ **At the interface between strategy design and execution are leadership and culture. The CEO can and should involve three leadership groups integral to a**

---

successful process: the strategy sponsors, the strategy team, and change agents.

❑ Change agents across the company may be managers or not; often they are key employees, opinion leaders and company boosters. They are the implementers. It is on their backs that strategy execution falls. Unless they own the strategy, fat chance.

❑ The crux of execution is people being accountable for achieving aligned-upon goals. Accountability is akin to pregnancy: Either you are 100 percent accountable, or you are not. Your results are the mirror.

❑ The CEO has to be a situational leader who adapts his or her leadership style to the respective Strategy-In-Action phase, his or her audience, and the needs of the company in each phase.

❑ For sustainable success, the organization's culture must match its strategy. A key tool for that is the incentive system. Unless the incentives are congruent with the strategy, there will be unintended results.

CHAPTER EIGHT

"Be The Change": Catalytic Actions

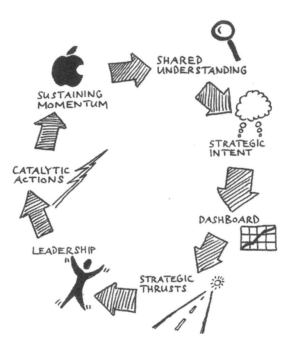

We shall never learn what "is called" swimming, for example,
or what it "calls for," by reading a treatise on swimming.
Only the leap into the river tells us what is called swimming.
Martin Heidegger

Case: IBM's Speed Team

Noblesse oblige: since IBM had catapulted the term "e-business" into the mainstream in the 1990s, the company felt honor-bound to remain the world's leading example of a fast-moving e-business. In short, IBM had to walk its talk. No, it had to *run* its talk. The leaders of the IT staff—a staggering 100,000 worldwide— knew IBM had great strengths, but also one big weakness, especially compared to the small and hungry competitors gnawing at the edges of its businesses: it was too cumbersome. "One of the things that frustrates me the most," said Steve Ward, VP of business transformation and chief information officer at IBM, "is the length of time between the 'aha' moment and the moment when you actually start changing the organization's direction, getting it to where it needs to be."

That was the birth of the Speed Team. Ward summoned 21 IBMers and gave them a simple assignment: get the IT group moving faster than ever, with a focus on rapid development of Web-based apps. Unlike many other companies, where the IT group is seen as a cost center and reports to the CFO, IBM's IT team was considered so crucial to the company's fortunes that Ward reported to J. Bruce Harreld, IBM's senior vice president of strategy and one of then-CEO Lou Gerstner's closest confidants. Translation: the Speed Team would be on the fast track. The team's co-leaders—Jane Harper, director of Internet technology and operations, and Ray Blair, director of e-procurement— had built strong reputations for pushing projects at a blazing pace. After talking to Ward about their mandate, the two leaders decided the team should have a finite life span—roughly six months. "I think that we will have failed if the Speed Team is still together three years from now," she explained.

Harper knew a thing or two about speed. She had been a key player in developing IBM's websites for high-profile events like Wimbledon and the U.S. Open, the Atlanta Olympic Games, and the chess match between Gary Kasparov and Deep Blue. By the early 2000s she ran, among other things, the 20-person WebAhead lab in Southbury, Connecticut, which prototyped new technologies.

The Speed Team wasted no time in mining the lab's culture for several of its key insights. WebAhead employees worked not in closed offices but in a single-office setup, not unlike that of a high-school computer lab: long tables of several employees arranged in rows. The overall atmosphere was informal, even messy. A sign on the door read, "THIS IS NOT YOUR FATHER'S IBM."

Once it had a number of fast-moving projects under its belt, the team examined what those projects had in common. It distilled six attributes of quick hits: strong leaders, team members who were "speed demons," clear objectives, a strong communication system, a carefully tailored process (not a one-size-fits-all approach), and a speed-oriented timetable.[96]

Initial results were encouraging, from the Video Watercooler for linking staffers in informal interactions like brainstorming or to share best practices, to a system for translating web data into phone data. But more than results, the best evidence of the Speed Team's success was that "our changes have been adopted by the organization," Blair said. "People have begun to think about the need for speed in their work. We're no longer necessary. Our job was to be catalysts, and catalysts can't linger around."

That is the operative word: catalyst. The essence of catalytic action lies in the famous words of Mahatma Gandhi, "Be today the change you wish the world to make." Catalytic actions are unlike linear action plans, which certainly have their rightful place. Action plans and catalytic projects work alongside each other; both have to co-exist, and both are crucial for getting to the goal. The designing and launching of catalytic projects does not rule out schedules, milestones, sub-goals, budgets and the like. But in addition to sequential planning and PERT charts, successful execution requires bold actions that break business-as-usual. Why? Because "From a management point of view, speed is of the essence," said Carlos Ghosn after he had turned around Nissan. "When you arrive at a job, you have a limited amount of time when people are willing to give you the benefit of the doubt. Also, Nissan's situation did not allow us to take a long time."[97] Once Ghosn had done the active listening he described in Chapter 3, he could move with the lightning speed essential for catalytic action.

Catalytic projects are typically 100-day mini-ventures designed to prove the validity of the strategy so they can be scaled up if they succeed. They should be low-cost and low-risk lest they jeopardize the whole company should they fail. But the strategy team should throw enough resources at each catalytic project and make it enough of a priority so the project can act as a pressure-cooker for altering the landscape of what is possible. By providing rapid feedback to the strategy, the new landscape of possibility will then inform—and transform—the strategic process.

If your strategy falls short of the mark, but represents progress in the right direction, is it better to execute now, or to interrupt the process and re-work the plan so it is closer to the mark? There is a saying by the eighteenth-century writer and researcher Johann Wolfgang von Goethe: "Whatever you can do, or dream you can, begin it. Boldness has genius, power, and magic in it." Better to take action now than to wait for the perfect strategy. A great advantage of Strategy-In-Action is the ongoing process. You will have the opportunity, after the 100-day catalytic project, to re-tune the strategy out of the action.

Separately and together, we have helped design, launch, and implement hundreds of catalytic projects, from developing and bringing to market a new simulation software to building the cross-cultural management competencies for 5,000 IT employees; from cleaning up a slum in Haiti's Carrefour area to introducing e-governance in Eastern Europe and Arab countries; and from producing 5 million euro through new product sales at a multinational energy company to launching a Brazilian restaurant in Harlem. This chapter tells the stories and, more importantly, aims to come up with best (and worst) practices.

Cutting Through Business-As-Usual

Business-as-usual can take many forms, including the desire to do everything as it's been done before; risk aversion, avoidance, apathy, resignation, or skepticism against new approaches, ideas or methods. Sometimes the status quo persists simply because of the sheer force of existing rules, behaviors or culture. Just like a big cruise ship at sea, turning around an organization is done a few degrees at a time. What can change the course of a large boat? Its trim tab. The architect, inventor, designer and futurist R. Buckminster Fuller said in a 1972 *Playboy* interview:

> Something hit me very hard once, thinking about what one little man could do. Think of the Queen Mary—the whole ship goes by and then comes the rudder. And there's a tiny thing at the edge of the rudder called a trim tab.
> It's a miniature rudder. Just moving the little trim tab builds a low pressure that pulls the rudder around. Takes almost no effort at all... the fact is that you can just put your foot out like that and the whole big ship of state is going to go.
> So I said, call me Trim Tab.[98]

"Little individuals" have the power to make a difference through catalytic actions—small, highly focused activities and clear, concise, measurable results that can ultimately turn the ship. They move the immovable when there is a need to act, take calculated risks, and score quick wins that build momentum. Success breeds success; the faster the team gets results along the strategic objectives, the faster it can change the landscape of what is possible. The key is to find that little trim tab.

That is what Salam Fayyad did long before he became prime minister. As finance minister of the Palestinian Authority in the 1990s, Fayyad faced a bureaucracy riddled with corruption, the type of graft that had allowed Yasser Arafat to funnel millions of dollars to his wife Suha in Paris. One example of the corruption was that many of the 53,000 Palestinian police officers named their relatives—brothers, cousins, uncles—as fake police officers to jack up their salaries, at a monthly cost of $20 million. How could they get away with that? What made the corruption possible was an economy based almost entirely on cash. Once Fayyad realized this, he found the trim tab. He made one simple change: He issued a rule that all wages would be transferred to bank accounts. There would be no more cash payments to police officers; to receive their monthly paycheck, each cop would need a bank account into which the Palestinian Authority would make direct deposits.[99] This changed everything. Since a fictitious person cannot open a bank account, from one month to the next, there were no more "ghost" police officers who looted the Palestinian treasury.

Typical catalytic actions are of two types. *Ground-breaking projects* explore innovative ways of achieving strategic objectives, such as Fayyad's coup with the Palestinian police force or Toyota's development of the Hybrid automobile or Google's Chrome word-processing software. When THP helped change the law in India so that women, who cannot inherit land (since usually the eldest brother inherits the whole lot from his father), could still get bank loans to build businesses without needing land as collateral, this broke entirely new ground: it transformed the economy, not to speak of women's leadership and self-image. When one company's European sales slackened because of a lack of ergonomic design in its handheld product line, a design team was assigned to address the issue, a single new ergonomic product was released into the European market, the response was good, the rest of the product line was retrofitted, and European sales grew.

The second type, *Proof-of-principle projects*, demonstrates with sufficient authority that successful innovations can be scaled up or serve as the basis for strategic decisions. When Ed went into the label conversion plant and saw the three-step process of three separate workstations all spewing start-up waste, he came up with the idea to streamline it into one continuous single-machine process with only one set-up making waste. He did not start out by converting the whole plant; he launched a pilot to prove the concept. Once the catalytic action had proved successful, the rest of the plant was rapidly converted. The results improved gross margins (by 14 points), on-time delivery and product quality.

Either way, catalytic actions are a low-cost and low-risk tool for companies to jumpstart the future, learn from the action, and feed the results back into strategy design. And if they work out, catalytic projects accelerate results, lower sunk costs, and ease the risks of innovation.

Catalytic actions typically focus on at least one of three things. One, they can fill gaps in existing programs or services, for example when a simulation software is not offered in a key market like Japan, when customer service is weak, or when an engineering team loses one day for each day it budgeted to build a satellite. Two, they can minimize duplication of efforts to save resources, for example when quality assurance testing is done for two different products separately but could be done together, or when in a space exploration company the optics teams of Germany and France were working separately and reinvented the wheel, and the catalytic project was to merge them so they learned from each other and eliminated redundancies. Three, they can seize opportunities for synergy to spark further improvements, for example when a survey of past customers could integrate with sales to maximize repeat business. No matter which focus, their aim is the same: to interrupt business-as-usual and make the future happen now.

Rule 1: In the Customer's Shoes

The ground rules for catalytic actions are simple. There are six of them. First, it pays rich dividends to stand in the shoes of the customer.

Case: Cemex and Innovative Home Financing

To better understand the service gaps for Mexico's less-affluent customers, Cemex recruited a team of employees to spend ten hours each day for a whole year in a dirt-poor neighborhood of Guadalajara. They learned that most inhabitants did not buy already-mixed (more expensive) concrete delivered by trucks, but rather the (less expensive) powdered cement in bags. The team also discovered that the act of building meant more to people than simply living space for them and their families. It meant *patrimonio*, an enduring legacy that people passed on to the next generation.

Another lesson for the Cemex team in Guadalajara was that people faced barriers in securing loans for their construction, since banks did not quite trust them and saw them as bad credit. They witnessed a unique approach to raising capital: poor Mexicans organized *tandas*, lotteries where each week a group of families put a specific sum into a common pool, and one lucky family won the whole pot at the end of the week. Although these funds were meant for building projects, many poor families used the winnings for other purposes like weddings and festivals.

So Cemex launched a catalytic project that galvanized community organizers to establish similar financing pools—but instead of cash, the winners received building materials, including cement. In addition, Cemex provided blueprints and construction advice to the winners. By 2003, the program had helped more than 30,000 families;[100] by 2008, 260,000 families had built or improved their homes through "Patrimonio Hoy." The catalytic action had started in one resource-poor neighborhood at the periphery of Cemex's activities; in a few months it had transformed how Cemex does business.

Rule 2: Rapid Results

The second ground rule: to build confidence and a sense of accomplishment, pick low-hanging fruit first. The idea is to score quick wins that boost the morale of the troops and allow for rapid-fire feedback from the action back to the strategy. That is why the typical timeframe for a catalytic project is 100 days. On the other hand, 100 days is not the bible; the Cemex projects lasted quite a bit longer. Choose a timeframe that serves as a milestone given the company's imperatives, that boxes people in, but that lets them see the light at the end of the tunnel, since catalytic actions are labor-intensive and can be exhausting. At one military contractor, the strategy team carried out six catalytic projects over 100 days:

- *Build rail simulator using next generation IG solution.*
- *Produce working, production-ready example of a Humvee vehicle/army simulator for demo purposes.*
- *Have a military Use-of-Force product at I/ITSEC.*
- *Profitability Mix: Get out of the leasing business.*
- *Deliver independently tested, zero-defect product "out the door."*
- *Push IES Warranty and Service. Have 10 customers sign on.*

Another, even faster example is the World Bank's Development Marketplace[101], a bi-annual event held since 1998 to capture innovative solutions for fighting poverty. It's almost like speed dating: the forum, held in the atrium at the World Bank's Washington headquarters, connects providers of innovative ideas of social entrepreneurs—not only from Bank staff, but anyone, anywhere—with potential funders. Speed was built into every facet of the process: since many applicants had impressive ideas but no funds to travel to Washington, the event team held teleconferences with 52 proposal teams from countries such as Egypt, Uganda, or the Philippines so they too could present their ideas to the jury. The panel of judges deciding on the grants included respected leaders of NGOs like Oxfam International and World Vision; executives of private-sector companies such as Asea Brown Boveri (ABB) and Battelle; and senior World Bank executives. At another forum in February 2002, the judges quickly distributed a pool of $5 million among 43 competitors for micro-funding; grants ranged from $29,000 to $380,000. After these catalytic projects, the process scaled up and decentralized: Country Innovation Days were held in Thailand, Peru, Ukraine, Brazil, and Guatemala.[102] For Development Marketplace 2009, applicants numbered 1,755; 100 finalists were awarded rapid seed money.

Rule 3: The Mantra "What Could Go Wrong?"

The third ground rule, "What could go wrong?" is one of the best questions the strategy team can ask to foresee and steer clear of future breakdowns. At a global financial institution, the strategy team saw that several things might go wrong: since it used to be a Swiss institution that merged with a U.S. investment bank, many people's English skills might be insufficient for collaborating on a global scale; a silo mentality blocked open communication; senior managers built their own turf rather than collaborating with other silos; people kept their knowledge or best practices from other silos. Senior managers also failed to communicate a clear vision, strategy or roadmap; the strategy got lost in the day-to-day; the knowledge workers mistrusted senior and top management; whatever the bosses said, the workers did not see them as credible. The strategy team came up with a set of catalytic actions to make up for these possible breakdowns:

- *Create communication strategy, communication plan, and "IT COE deck" which can be reused for all communication purposes (e.g., town halls).*
- *Include change management targets into performance review process.*
- *Establish change management and cross-cultural education and train EMT members, leverage business school.*
- *Establish focus groups for IT COE in order to engage employees, create a common language and create a two-way communication, potential use to support implementation of other catalytic projects.*
- *Enhance use of and experiment with collaboration technologies.*
- *Identify and train key ambassadors; strengthen English language skills.*

Rule 4: Low-Cost, Low-Risk

The fourth ground rule bears repeating: catalytic projects should be both low-risk and low-cost so they don't sink the boat if—despite the team's best efforts—they should fail. They serve as pathways to major change, but minimize the risk and cost of such change by creating a controlled, manageable environment in which new concepts can be developed and tested. 150 senior leaders at a space aviation company launched 28 low-cost and low-risk catalytic pilots, with four to six managers joining each project. One project aimed to reduce time slippage on satellite assembly, which had been one day lost for every day budgeted—in other words, 100 percent slippage. With a satellite build time of three to five years, you can guess how expensive such slippage is, not to speak of reputation costs (what does the customer think when a product is months late?). So the team launched a catalytic project to reduce slippage in two satellite programs. In one they ended up cutting the delays from 100 percent to 30 percent, in the other to 10 percent. The beauty was, they did this at virtually no cost or risk (other than weekly meetings to check progress, communicate successes, remove barriers, and coordinate for action).

Rule 5: A New Quality of Life

Fifth, catalytic projects must be visionary, meaning their achievement will offer a new quality of life for the players, their department, and/ or the company as a whole. In India, catalytic projects focused on establishing "hunger-free zones" as islands of success that would point to a future free from hunger. In eight countries in Africa, THP mobilized 105 "epicenters": clusters of rural villages where women and men ran their own programs to meet basic needs. They might build a community training center with bricks they pressed themselves. They might learn literacy and new skills in income-generating activities. They might coordinate their own local strategies for food production, handicrafts, or food storage. They might organize their own rural bank for savings and microcredit. After a five-year period, an epicenter became completely self-reliant—it funded its own activities and no longer needed outside funding. As of 2009, eighteen epicenters were self-reliant, economically viable, and environmentally sustainable.[103] Rarely had the essence of catalytic projects been put across more vividly than by the hundreds of thousands of India's and Africa's local leaders who took charge of their own quality of life.

Rule 6: Measurable, Unconditional, Unpredictable, Visionary

Sixth and last, catalytic project goals must be clearly measurable so the players know exactly where they are at all times, and there is no ambiguity about winning or losing. A high-tech company in the Middle East set itself the goal to get ten dental schools in the United States to use its simulation product in training their students. THP and the Planning Commission of India launched one catalytic project that focused on training 67,000 village officials—men and women—to be effective "animators" or change agents in ending hunger. Project goals must be unconditional, meaning not dependent on particular circumstances or conditions like "we'll do it if we get the budget for it." They must be unpredictable, meaning a breakthrough and departure from past performance. Just a few years ago, Nokia faced troubles in the key emerging market China. It trailed market leader Motorola; worse, it was threatened by local upstarts like TCL and Ningbo Bird that flooded stores nationwide with armies of sales reps flogging their brands. "Our people would put up posters, and within 30 minutes they would be torn down," recalled Colin Giles, now Nokia's global head of sales and at the time manager of its China handset business. Visiting a shop in the western city of Chengdu, Giles said, "you could hardly move in the store because of the number of salespeople." With their people power and their inexpensive but well-designed mobiles, the newcomers had quickly gobbled up almost half the market.

Giles fought back and pushed through several catalytic changes. Nokia decentralized, going from three Chinese sales offices in 2003 to 70 and from eight national distributors to 50 provincial ones. Since rivals were having great success with handsets designed for mainland users, Nokia introduced its own China-specific models. For instance, many rural Chinese were unfamiliar with the romanized transliteration system that most cell phones use to input Chinese for text messages, so Nokia developed two phones with software that let users write characters with a stylus. The result: By 2005 Nokia sold 27.5 million handsets in China, triple what it had sold in 2003.[104] It was clearly the top brand, and not only in China: by 2010 Nokia held 35 percent of the world market, and the number of Nokia devices in use was more than one billion. (In the years since, the company has lost market share in an extremely crowded and competitive field.) The difference: the guts to take catalytic actions that were not bound by circumstances, not reasonable, and not predictable.

Failure Adds Value Too

Catalytic projects can be either quick wins *or* quick losses; either allows for rapid feedback to the strategy. "Steve Jobs is a case in point," said Robert Sutton, a professor of management science and engineering at Stanford University's School of Engineering. "Everyone seems to recall the great things he has done, yet he made lots of mistakes, too. The Apple III. The Lisa, which was a financial flop. Next, the Mac Cube. But he pulls the plug quickly when he realizes something isn't working." Sutton immediately added, "I don't mean to say that the strategy itself is unimportant. I just think that too much emphasis is placed on bearing the child versus raising the child. A well-executed 'good enough' strategy will beat a poorly executed brilliant strategy every time."[105]

And failure can be as instructive as success. Today, one of the best companies at harnessing failures for innovation is Google. "Fundamentally, everything we do is experiment," said Douglas Merrill, a Google vice president for engineering. "The thing with experimentation is that you have to get data and then be brutally honest assessing it." When Google introduces new features, it has stayed true to a "fail fast" strategy: launch, listen, improve, launch again. When Google Answers, a multi-million dollar, four-year effort to build an expert answer service, failed and the company had to shut it down in late 2006, Merrill preferred to see even that failure as an experiment that yielded useful knowledge. "I don't think Answers was a failure, because we incorporated a lot of what we learned into our new custom search engine."[106] And that is the point: The only real disasters are the ones where you don't learn anything. Without the freedom to come up with ill-conceived initiatives, Google might have never become the hot and highly profitable company it is today, and Apple might have never brought about commercial breakthroughs from iTunes to iPhone and iPad that have gone mainstream. Catalytic projects must offer the freedom to fail. We couldn't express the spirit of catalytic action any better than former U.S. president Theodore Roosevelt and will close this chapter with his stirring words.

> It is not the critic who counts: not the man who points out how the strong man stumbles or where the doer of deeds could have done better. The credit belongs to the man who is actually in the arena, whose face is marred by dust and sweat and blood, who strives valiantly, who errs and comes up short again and again, because there is no effort without error or shortcoming, but who knows the great enthusiasms, the great devotions, who spends himself for a worthy cause; who, at the best, knows, in the end, the triumph of high achievement, and who, at the worst, if he fails, at least he fails while daring greatly, so that his place shall never be with those cold and timid souls who knew neither victory nor defeat.[107]

∾

Boiling It Down

❑ Catalytic projects are *not* traditional action plans, which have their place but would be too linear for achieving a bold vision. Catalytic actions are low-cost, low-risk pressure-cookers designed to transform the landscape of what is possible and to provide rapid feedback from the action back to the strategy design (hence the name Strategy-In-Action). The best strategies are matched with bold, catalytic actions that jump-start implementation, produce quick wins, and can be scaled up if successful.

❑ Catalytic actions are either proof-of-concept or ground-breaking pilots. They typically focus on one or more of four things: filling gaps in existing programs or services; minimizing duplication of efforts to save resources; achieving convergence of existing initiatives; and/or seizing opportunities for synergy to spark further improvement.

❑ Catalytic actions are pathways for making major changes while controlling risk and cost through a fixed, manageable environment in which the new concepts can be tested. Even failure can provide useful learning that improves the strategy.

❑ The ground rules for catalytic actions are: Pick easy actions first, to build and strengthen confidence and a sense of accomplishment. Ask, "What could go wrong?" to anticipate and prevent future breakdowns. Catalyze rapid-fire successes, usually through bold promises and requests.

❑ Catalytic project goals must be measurable (not vague activities but specific outcomes), unconditional (not dependent on circumstances or conditions), unpredictable (a departure from past performance), and visionary (leading to a new future for the stakeholders, the department, the company or society).

CHAPTER NINE

Sustaining Momentum: Feedback, Standards, Scale-Up

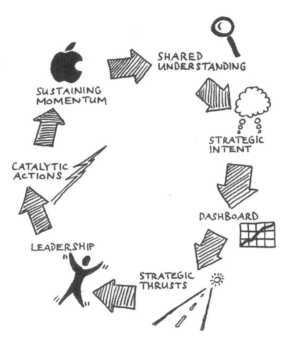

The more precise the measurement of position,
the more imprecise the measurement of momentum,
and vice versa.

Werner von Heisenberg

Now that the 100-day catalytic projects are done, we come to the final building block of Strategy-In-Action, a phase often overlooked by planners: consolidation, re-evaluation, standardization, and rollout to the whole company. The team has won an important battle and planted the flag; now the beachhead must be held and expanded to win the war. The issue now is, in one word, sustainability.

A Dynamic Feedback Loop

How can you sustain and expand success? The strategy team looks at intended as well as unintended outcomes from the catalytic projects and feeds its insights back into the strategy. Real-time feedback allows strategists to see and provide what's missing, and in the aftermath of action adapt the strategy to the new landscape. Participants take stock, learn from innovations elsewhere, engage others, and enrich the strategy for the next round.

An action can yield one of three outcomes: either it achieves all its intended results, or some, or none at all. In Strategy-In-Action, timely and accurate feedback is crucial; as results come in, the strategy team evaluates them. If they match the objectives, the team reinforces or standardizes the actions. If they fail to match, a hard look at the strategic assumptions, objectives or activities is in order.

This dynamic does not happen automatically, or only once. Strategy-In-Action is, in the metaphor of C.K. Prahalad and Gary Hamel, like running a marathon in a series of sprints.[108] It is a dialectic process that drives continuous improvement. It means investing the time and paying the opportunity costs in stepping back periodically to refresh the unvarnished look on the organization, its environment, objectives, actions, and results. The company remains vigilant; its stakeholders know that strategies and organizations, industries and markets are all moving targets. Like in white-water rafting (we prefer this metaphor to the marathon metaphor above, since in river rafting conditions change constantly and you have to be extremely flexible and change your plan at a moment's notice), strategists need a willingness to be simultaneously in and out of control, be open to where the river takes them, but never lose sight of the prize.

In its heyday Nokia stepped back each year as a whole company through the "Annual Nokia Way" when it asked each office worldwide at the end of the year to analyze its results and the current reality, come up with strategic recommendations based on its experiences in the field, and send those to headquarters in Helsinki, which carefully reviewed them and integrated them in its comprehensive global strategy for the next year.

Board and management can use six tools for sustaining momentum: most important—to repeat Jack Welch's words—communicate, communicate, communicate; but also debriefing, monitoring, visual displays, reassessment and realignment, and streamlining. We review each of these tools in turn. All of them are essential for the ultimate aim of this phase: standardizing and scale-up. And perhaps the company will reach the holy grail of organizational life: being a *strategic organization*.

Communicate, Communicate, Communicate

Without communication, strategy is useless. Nowhere is this truer than for sustaining momentum. Systematically communicating successes— and yes, failures—to the right stakeholders is as important as those successes and failures themselves. Mahatma Gandhi's salt march is a superb example of capitalizing on a simple result for a vast strategy. In 1930, Gandhi led a march of several thousand Indians from Ahmadabad to the Arabian Sea, where the frail man bent down slowly, dipped into the water, and cupped a little salt in his hand.

By itself, the salt march was hardly the stuff from which revolutions are made. It was one man walking 320 kilometers (some 200 miles) with a few thousand followers, a tiny number relative to India's population. So why did that walk alter history? Gandhi was sly: he had a knack for the symbolic meaning of actions, and he knew that his tiny feat, cupping a handful of seawater, was an unthinkable act for an Indian. None of the onlookers mistook the signal either: Producing salt from seawater was an act of defiance against the British colonial power, which alone enjoyed the privilege of refining salt and extracting a "salt tax" from its Indian subjects. The march's strategic value came with the communication surrounding it: its unmistakable message of insubordination infuriated the British colonial power and inspired millions of Indians to question the status quo. That message made the salt march an historic moment and shifted the political environment in India and the British Empire. And all that had been brought about by one little man in a loincloth and a handful of salt.

Gandhi's brilliance was not only the salt march itself, but how he turned it into a global PR message—without email or Twitter—that helped achieve India's freedom from the British Empire. The strategy team may not be as cunning as Gandhi, but it can, and must, still exploit its communications for the greatest impact. During the sustainability phase it must be two-headed: communicate successes *and* failures internally, for example to employees and the board, and communicate successes externally, for example to investors and the media. Communication must be frequent and continuous. The team can use several types: updates; big-picture contextual messages; and two-way communications. The first type makes progress (and/or barriers) visible to change agents and ultimately to all stakeholders. Updates are typically one-way communications from the CEO, reinforced by the strategy team in all its messages. These messages go out frequently across the organization and may be tailored to each audience, but the leadership team stays on message. They can be internal newsletters, email blasts or webcasts, for example when a "hero" employee has produced an extraordinary result that points the direction of the strategy.

The second type, big-picture contextual messages, are communications from the CEO and strategy team to paint the day-to-day tackling into a strategic context, show leadership by example, or give reasons for strategic decisions.

Many years ago, our fellow strategist Tapas K. Sen reminded a CEO of the importance of the third type, two-way communication. The CEO grew quite irritated. "Of course I do two-way communication," he snapped at Dr. Sen. "I write to my people, and I talk to my people!" He had missed the other, crucial dimension of two-way communication: listening and getting feedback. For a proactive, ongoing, and authentic discussion of strategy at multiple company levels, be sure you are truly interested in what your stakeholders have to say. Stakeholders are smart, so they will feel if you say "dialogue" but really mean "monologue." On the other hand, they will feel part of the game if two-way communication features three crucial components. One is guaranteed confidentiality and assurances that nobody will be punished for talking straight. Another is a proactive board and strategy team that request feedback from employees, customers, and other stakeholders. And a third is prompt and impeccable follow-up on all promises and requests so that stakeholders see that their feedback is taken seriously and makes a difference. Unless the leadership team is willing to heed these three ground rules, the two-way communication will likely turn into an empty alibi and a wasted effort.

The feedback sensing system consists of market feedback, customer feedback, and employee feedback. Measurement both on a real-time and longitudinal basis affords feedback on strategic status, progress, and impact. The strategy team should commit the resources to getting this feedback systematically and frequently. Above all, board and management must keep up their commitment to a participatory process—which now means not merely to tolerate feedback but to pull for it; and not only to listen to feedback but also to act on it. Such responsiveness should not be confused with knee-jerk reactions. It is a measured and systematic response within a strategy context. And it is a stance that turns the company from reactive to proactive.

Debriefing

At the global bank that engaged in Strategy-In-Action, the results of the eight catalytic projects exceeded company leaders' expectations and was one of the factors that contributed to the firm's saving $200 million and achieving $9 billion profit that year. A great result, but not enough for ongoing success; company leaders needed to do it again and again. That is what sustaining the momentum is about: feeding insights from the action back into the strategy. In a debrief session, the strategy team looked at the new landscape produced by the catalytic actions. Their department had transformed from what it had been even a few months before. The quality of the work—the tenor of the meetings, the deepened trust among team members, the straight talk and open communication, the collaboration and knowledge-sharing with other departments, the speed of decisions, the fun—was barely recognizable. The stakeholders had learned a lot about how to—and how not to—facilitate change. Now the team distilled the key lessons, best practices, and success factors, and circulated them in a slide deck so the next time around their colleagues could stand on their shoulders:

- *Change management has to be contributed top down. The senior management first has to build a common understanding of the mechanics of changes and then has to* **commonly** *develop an appropriate approach.*
- *It is vital to understand one's own (country & divisional) culture to start a* **dialogue** *with other cultures. This is a precondition to start discussion about a common culture.*
- *The strategic intent has to be crystal clear to each and every employee. Top down* **communication** *must be strongly encouraged.*
- *Mastering change is mainly based on the capability to handle a* **non-linear process** *and* **emotions**. *Building this competency takes time and requires resources (it is not god-given—and it is not a shame not having it). Change can be steered but not managed and measured as other business processes.*
- **Trust** *is built on actions and not on words—walk the talk!*
- *Change Management is mainly handled with same instruments as day to day business and projects—but it is different.*
- *Providing tools and checklists is by far not sufficient for successfully mastering the change—it is people business and people business is about relationship.*
- *Every major change causes specific behavior and strong emotions—this is true for staff as well as for management. An average IT manager is an expert with engineering approaches—but not with emotional reactions.*
- *There is no common understanding of how a change happens and what interventions could be used to steer the change—but this would be vital for mastering the change.*

- *Change Management should not be a bottom up approach—top management has to actively support and contribute. Besides the country-specific culture, there are divisional cultures—pretty often people are not aware of their own culture. It is difficult to change if the current state is not known (where to start?).*
- *People need to have a direction in times of changes—otherwise they don't know where to go. Currently there is no explicit perspective (strategic intent) communicated by top management.*

Such debriefs are valuable, even essential for sustaining momentum. It is just like in war: after each mission, debriefs are about fine-tuning the strategy and ultimately winning the war. Without debriefing every key initiative, the company will miss out on key intelligence, reinvent the wheel over and over again, or waste valuable resources—in time, treasure, or lives. When we debrief, we usually ask six simple questions: What was accomplished (along the company goals)? What was not accomplished? What worked? What did not work? What leaders emerged, and how can they be empowered now? What opportunities emerged? And based on the answers to these questions, what's next?

Ongoing Dashboard

We saw in Chapter 5 that your metrics are key to your strategy; whatever you measure will run your life. In other words, the indicators you choose will shape what you see, how you see it, and the actions you take based on your perception. Now we add: You are never done measuring. It is not something you can tick off on your checklist. You have to keep up your vigilance so your monitoring doesn't veer off track. Every troubled company we have gone into used multiple measurement systems and spent a lot of time arguing about which data was correct and which wasn't. The way around this is to align on one system and to accept the data that system yields as valid and actionable (at least until the next round of shared understanding). This prevents the manipulation of statistics in support of one position or another, or the use of statistics as a smokescreen to hide from reality. (Remember the adage that "There are three kinds of lies: lies, damned lies, and statistics"?[109])

One way to get systematic feedback is the Balanced Scorecard (BSC). Robert B. Harris, then-senior vice president of strategy at the Toronto-based healthcare and life sciences provider MDS, said in an interview with Harvard Business School that he saw the timely adoption of a Balanced Scorecard approach as a key success factor in building the MDS into a $100 billion company. (The company's approach was so low-key that *Good to Great* author Jim Collins quipped MDS' apparent goal was to become the world's least-heard-of $100 billion company.) "We had already defined our goals," Harris said; "now we needed to get every-one regularly talking about how to achieve our strategic objectives." And why did he prefer the BSC approach to traditional metrics? "The BSC al-lows us to focus on action. With the BSC, we hope to increase the amount of time that senior management spends on strategic decision making. In addition, because we use BSC software, we can electronically connect every employee back to the strategy."[110] *Connect every employee back to the strategy.* Whether or not you use BSC, that is the key. And one of the most potent tools in calling forth stakeholders' committed action consis-tent with the strategy are visual displays.

Visual Displays

Productivity is a function not merely of commitment, which can be as-sumed (a stakeholder without commitment does not deserve the name), but of the right displays staring team members in the face. Displays are vital for charting progress, building confidence, and succeeding in any endeavor. The right displays will compel people to focus on the highest-leverage actions in service of the strategic intent.

Webster's defines *display* as "an exhibit, a manifestation, anything that is displayed or shown or revealed." Many people think of displays as spreadsheets, checklists, schedules, or PERT charts. But that's not the whole story. Displays can include graphs, reminders, inspiring quotes, or visuals such as photographs or YouTube videos. They can be as small as an e-mail bulletin or a Blackberry memo, or as large as a flipchart page or a poster that covers an office wall. Used in this sense, a display is a visual representation of what the company is committed to, telling teams where they are in meeting key goals, what's missing, and what's next, and pulling for decisive action. Such a display might not look like a spreadsheet, which inspires few people. Instead, you can see your entire environment—the office, the desk, the time planner, the computer screen, the smart-phone, the meeting rooms, even the company car—as a set of displays that can remind stakeholders of the bigger picture, compel them to take certain actions, and support them in meeting the strategic intent.

For the president of a family-owned company, his office door was a compelling part of his display—unfortunately, we might add. His boss, the chairman, used to stick his head into the president's office whenever he so pleased, or summon him at a moment's notice. The open door pulled for certain actions and ruled out others. Displays run your life. In other words, whatever—and whoever—is in your face tends to dictate what you do and what you don't do. If your office is cluttered, that clutter is its own display that will pull for the actions you take—even the actions you can *think* of taking. Because of the clutter, you do things you simply would not do in a well-ordered environment. You lose half an hour searching for that crucial file. You focus on whatever is on top of the stack, no matter what the priority is. There is no distinction between urgent and important; everything has equal priority until a crisis hits; whatever is most urgent gets done first. Things fall through the cracks. (And don't think we just say so because Thomas is Swiss; clutter really *is* a waste.)

The choice is yours. You can either shape your environment, or you can choose not to shape it, in which case it will be shaped by the drift of the circumstances. There is always a display around you; the trick is to go about it deliberately, to display just enough of the right data in the right style so people take the actions that get the desired outcomes.

Committed to improving its customer service, Citibank Privatkunden AG in Germany set itself two benchmarks. One, it sought to cut waiting time for customers calling in from 20 seconds to 8 seconds; two, each bank manager took five minutes each day to achieve a "wow" effect by exceeding a customer's expectations. Results and highlights for these intentions were displayed frequently to branch managers and employees on flipcharts. Bank executives also discovered two additional displays: They found that their call-center people were more personable on the phone if they could drink coffee at their desks and if they looked into a mirror while talking to customers on the phone. In this case, flipcharts, mirrors, and coffee were the key displays enhancing performance.

Displays can be imaginative and fun. In one end-of-the-year campaign, one organization spread balloons all around the office, people wore crazy hats, and each had a whistle to blow whenever a funding pledge came in. (Okay, we agree, that might strike some as overly "American.") A big chart on the wall showed a thermometer, with pledges in green and revenues in blue. These displays were designed to shift the atmosphere from seriousness and worrying about the goal's feasibility to bold, playful action and the joy of results. It was a ball, and it worked: in that campaign, the organization delivered a 17-percent increase in fundraising over the previous year.

Given your strategic intent, what information do you need around you? Who else needs to see the display so that it pulls for their strategic actions and behaviors (the strategy team, other stakeholders)? How often do you and team members need to review the display (monthly, weekly, daily)? In what format should it be displayed (on paper or electronically, visually or numbers, in the office or on a server)? A display managed—or at least seen—by other stakeholders can "force" implementers to live up to the strategic intent in the day-to-day. If your managers lose sight of the big picture in the heat of urgent business, a compelling display of the strategic intent and key metrics will help keep the big picture on people's radar.

Reassessment and Realignment

Periodically, for instance each quarter, the strategy team should hold a formal meeting to assess progress and results, with a probing discussion on the strategy. This strategic wellness-check should happen at the leadership level. It should not dwell on past performance but on the new landscape made available by the catalytic actions, the implications for strategy, and the options for improving future performance. Managers should schedule meetings in the right sequence to facilitate the flow of knowledge from lower to higher levels. Lower-level reporting meetings should come prior to higher-level unit or division meetings. Two to four hours for both lower-level and leadership meetings are ideal.

Perhaps annually or every eighteen months, the strategy team should revisit the entire strategy. Organizations, industries, and markets are all in flux, and strategies or actions might be complete or in need of updating. It is time to take a fresh unvarnished look, see if the thrusts are still the best paths to the strategic intent, and realign them if needed. Since all strategy team members have been steeped in the Strategy-In-Action methodology and participated in the strategy design, this checkup is much easier than it would be in a top-down strategy process. Still, issues might come up, such as dependencies on other departments, joint ownership of objectives, differences over budgets and resource levels, or resistance to being held accountable. The team should not belittle or bulldoze such issues, or they can throw a monkey wrench into the process.

The ongoing and visible commitment of the strategy sponsors—in a public company that means board commitment—to the process is crucial for sustaining success. Top management should display the strategy highlights to the board regularly, ideally with the strategy team present (and presenting). When we work with a company's board, we use an executive presentation template for each board meeting. Displaying the strategy, objectives, catalytic actions, and strategic results in no more than three to five slides, we aim to provide a platform for high-level discussion, maximize the bird's eye view board members need, and maintain alignment between board and management.

Streamlining

One pitfall of involving multiple stakeholders is this: the action can get so complex that it loses momentum. At a major pharmaceutical company, the CEO realized that he was separated from the frontline employees by too many layers. When he challenged the leadership team to flatten the organization, some division heads were surprised to discover several more layers than they had thought—as many as fourteen in one case. The organizational structure had taken on a life of its own. The leadership team agreed to consolidate down to eight layers maximum.

Case: Streamlining at ConAgra

The streamlining with the richest dividends is done as a co-creation. When ConAgra reorganized its enterprise functions and brand groups, it uncovered a set of processes that would have made the Tower of Babel pale in comparison.[111] Each function and brand produced sales reports with massive amounts of data that ran hundreds of pages, but finance could not analyze them because each brand counted different units of sale—pounds, pallets, cartons, dollars, shipments, cans, and so on. Supply chain managers had to negotiate purchases in dozens of can sizes that required different vendors and manufacturing. Even ingredients were overly complex: to use but one example, the company was using twelve different types of carrots.

To simplify, ConAgra's CEO Gary Rodkin and his senior management team introduced an initiative called RoadMap, designed to bring together people from across the company to redesign critical processes. For two days, representatives of the consumer brand operating groups, the commercial businesses, and the enterprise functions—a total of more than 60 people—debated these standards with a simple ground rule: by the end of the second day they would, by hook or by crook, align on a single procedure by which they would all live. And if they could not reach a decision, the CEO or CFO would intervene and decide for them. As it turned out, the group did reach consensus, which allowed finance and IT to spend the next few months building a company-wide reporting system.

The savings were substantial. In the Canadian division, the effort focused on simplifying ways of managing discontinued products, ordering raw and packaging materials, and tracking inventory write-offs by $1.5 million. By this point more than 1,000 ConAgra employees had participated in streamlining initiatives. A culture of simplicity had begun. Rodkin reinforced that culture by setting specific cost-reduction targets tied to eliminating duplication, and by publicly declaring simplicity as a key priority and a performance review criterion for managers.

To walk his talk and lead by example, Rodkin invited his senior team to suggest how he himself could manage more simply. One thing he learned was that he at times failed to specify which person should take the lead on a cross-functional or cross-unit issue. That created what the team called "jump balls": multiple executives assuming that they had the lead or that someone else did. Once Rodkin had reduced jump balls and simplified the resolution of critical issues, he realized that management teams the next level down copied his seemingly innocuous behavior and created redundant complexity there. So the impact of simplicity went far beyond Rodkin's and his top managers' behavior.

Standardizing and Scale-Up

The raison d'être of catalytic projects is that if they turn out, the team can standardize the success and scale up. For fifteen years, in countless catalytic projects (as we saw in Chapter 8), THP developed a replicable, affordable, bottom-up methodology that proved successful for overcoming poverty in rural areas of Africa, places so remote that politicians did not visit even during election campaigns. THP's "epicenter strategy" created dynamic centers for community action to meet basic needs and serve as focal points for linking people to government resources. Through four phases over five years, an epicenter takes people from abject poverty to self-reliance—at a cost of $8 per person per year. The first scale-up happened organically: by 2006, the epicenter strategy had empowered more than three million people to achieve lasting progress by building their own health centers, their own schools, literacy training, food security, banking, and family income.

The next challenge became taking these successful interventions to the national scale—in other words, to scale up again. The UN Millenium Project had come independently to the same conclusion. THP set out on a bold venture: to demonstrate that scale-up is possible in Africa, and that a bottom-up approach is a viable alternative for the entire continent. Scale-up included making best practices available at all epicenters, and subjecting the epicenters to state-of-the-art independent evaluation. It was a risky bet, since scale-up needed success in areas where humanity has often failed miserably—authentic partnership between women and men, effective collaboration among agencies, and bridging the gap between governments and people.

The risk paid off. By 2009, Hunger Project animators had mobilized rural communities at 108 epicenters in more than 1,000 villages in eight countries across Africa. Meanwhile in India and Bangladesh, THP had trained more than 90,000 village-level volunteers known as animators— in equal numbers women and men—and empowered them to lead a Vision, Commitment and Action Workshop and facilitate communities in achieving their own self-reliance. Animators led campaigns to build health centers, latrines, and schools, and to form cooperatives for boosting incomes.[112] The results by April 2009 in Uganda alone: 183,625 participants in THP's Vision, Commitment & Action Workshop, 20 tons of grain stored in epicenter food banks, 38 hectares of cassava planted, 1,000 kilos of nutritious porridge sold to schools and pregnant mothers, 4,000 kilos improved seed distributed, 83,000 participants in HIV/AIDS programs, 10,165 children immunized against killer diseases, water-borne illnesses reduced by 70 percent in the epicenters, and Ush 384.1 million ($178,651) disbursed as micro-credits to 992 "partners" (747 women and 245 men)[113]—the epitome of self-reliance and self-sustaining momentum.

A Strategic Organization

These results often made the difference between living in abject poverty and a dignified middle-class life for millions of people. But THP achieved something else that might be considered the holy grail of organizations: it became what development expert David C. Korten, whom we met in Chapter 2, has called a "strategic organization." Korten analyzed several types of organizations—relief organizations, development organizations, and a new kind. "The difference: A strategic organization is able to look beyond merely responding to existing circumstances or predictable opportunities. A strategic organization creates new opportunities, which otherwise might not occur; that is, it engages in the creation of its own future."[114] A strategic organization is totally unlike a traditional organization. Rather, it involves

> what Ansoff *et al.* labeled a "planning-learning process." The result is accurately described as "strategic organization," in which environmental surveillance and response capacities are linked and distributed throughout. Analytical and social processes are interrelated

such that all levels and units of the organization assume a strategic orientation, interacting dynamically with their environment within the guidelines of central policy and the values of a strong organizational culture.

In the strategic organization, senior managers have their work cut out for them:

The most important task of top management in a strategic organization is not the making of strategic decisions, but rather the development and maintenance of a total institutional capacity for strategic action.

Being a strategic organization is the essence any organization in any sector, from business to government to military, should strive for. The ideal is a convergence of strategic and day-to-day activities into one seamless set of actions that drive the organization forward. As the company masters this phase, it evolves into a strategy-driven entity. All of its actions, even the smallest, go through a strategic filter, nothing is done that is not strategic, and each day-to-day activity is imbued with strategic meaning. Feedback from strategic actions puts the organization on a self-correcting course to creating its own future—a future that might otherwise not occur.

In business, one outstanding example of a strategic organization is Amazon.com, called by *Forbes* "the General Electric of our times" and its founder Jeff Bezos "the Jack Welch."[115] Perhaps more than any other corporation, it embodies the emerging culture of strategy. Sure, there are other great companies in the technology space, such as Google, Apple, Facebook or Microsoft, whose greatness lies in their innovation or design; in corporate strategy, Amazon is the grandmaster that has systematically disrupted, taken down, and reinvented an entire industry. Witness the company's strategic actions over the past years (as told by *Forbes*).[116]

1. *One-click shopping*
2. *Free shipping over $25*
3. *Being first to market with a meaningful and usable, but predatory, offering for self-publishers (Amazon Advantage) at a time (late 90s) when getting traditional distribution as a small or self-publisher was nearly impossible*
4. *Creating a used-book marketplace that made used books go from 4% of the market to something like 30% in just a few years*
5. *Fighting a supply-chain battle with on-demand printers, using its 24-hour shipping model as a weapon to bring print volumes to Book Surge, its in-house operation*
6. *Undercutting Lulu, the pioneering self-publishing operation catering to authors, with its Createspace offering, which offers authors better margins*
7. *Booting up the Amazon Affiliate program (which, from unverified sources, accounts for about 40% of sales)*
8. *Making it brain-dead simple to publish on the Kindle*
9. *Creating a royalty option structure for Kindle publishers (70% between $2.99 and $9.99, 35% above $9.99) that leaves you with an offer you cannot refuse for the under-$9.99 price range*
10. *Once the traditional supply chain had been sufficiently weakened that traditional publishers were no longer very useful, ramping up direct relationships with authors*
11. *Starting with an eBook experience that was as close as possible to traditional books, but pushing the envelope as fast as readers could handle, towards more flexible digital formats (blogs on the Kindle, Kindle "singles," and with the recently announced capabilities of the Kindle format, high-quality graphics)*
12. *Decisively promoting a pawn (ebooks) to Queen with its book-lending model and recent offer-you-cannot-refuse for publishers who go Kindle-exclusive for at least the first 90 days (in the next year, we will likely see a shift towards an ebook-first or ebook-only strategy for many small publishers; so far, ebooks have been considered a "plus" market).*
13. *All the while, keeping the core shopping experience familiar, but pulling out all stops to increase conversions and same-visit sales with mechanisms ranging from book previews/searches to related-reading recommendations, and bundling recommendations*

This is far from theoretical. Many of these actions have affected us personally, as authors, over the past decade, and our lives have become inextricably linked to Amazon in more ways than one. Not only have we spent thousands of dollars and Euros on Amazon.com and Amazon.de; Thomas makes a significant portion of his income from Amazon in various regions (.com, .uk, .de, .fr, even .in and .au); he participated in Amazon Advantage and now on the Kindle Direct Publishing (KDP) platform.

Ultimately Amazon is not in the business of selling books, or selling other things, or even publishing. Amazon is in the business of innovating business models, in dozens of different ways; Amazon Web Services (AWS), the company's cloud computing platform, is but one of many. The Kindle Fire was another: designed with three-moves-ahead foresight, it incorporates the recognition that the cloud provisioning end is vastly more important to control than the device itself, since the money will ultimately move to content, as the hardware turns into a commodity. Watching Amazon is like watching a chess game unfold. At any given time the company seems to choose which game to play against which opponent, and then set about winning that game. And usually the game is won before opponents fully realize it has begun. You could say that Amazon is not offering a product in search of a business model, but a business model in search of a product. It is the strategic organization *par excellence*.

∼

Boiling It Down

❑ **The aim of sustaining momentum is to learn from the action: standardize what worked, eliminate what did not, spread best practices, and scale up.**

❑ **The six success factors in this phase are above all inclusive communication, and also debriefing, monitoring, displays, reassessment/realignment, streamlining, and standardizing/scale-up.**

❑ Communication on the strategic process must be ongoing and proactive. They can be updates or highlights; messages that put mundane activities into a big-picture context and meaning; or two-way communication to check the validity of the strategy, actions, or decisions.

❑ For strategy to be most effective it has to be integrated in the company's day-to-day operations. The ideal is the convergence of strategic and day-to-day activities into one seamless set of actions that drive the organization forward.

❑ The company stays on its toes since strategy, industry, and markets are all moving targets. Part of sustaining momentum is to step back periodically and refresh the unvarnished view of the company, environment, and objectives. Strategy and action are not suspended but reformulated in a self-correcting process of continuous improvement.

❑ The organization that has embedded Strategy-In-Action in its DNA is a "strategic organization" that does not merely respond to existing circumstances or opportunities, but engages in the creation of its own future and continually reinvents itself in the service of its strategic intent.

❑ The strategic organization is the holy grail of strategy. Its embodiment in the technology space is Amazon.

CHAPTER TEN

Troubleshooting: What to Do When...

Nothing is as good as one hopes,
and nothing
as bad as one fears.
Francois-René Chateaubriand

This book is designed as a reference guide that strategists can consult time and again in their ongoing quest for being a strategic organization. This chapter is an incomplete troubleshooting manual: It deals with some common problems that can arise in the heat of Strategy-In-Action. Of course it is virtually impossible to foresee, let alone cover, all possible candidates for troubleshooting. But you will find enough ideas and cross-references here to put together your own tactics for tackling the inevitable obstacles along the way.

From Breakdown to Breakthrough

The operative word here is "inevitable": when you go for a strategic intent that lies beyond the merely predictable, you and/or your colleagues *will* run into walls. Breakdowns come with the territory of Stategy-In-Action; failures will happen and some strategic actions will come to naught. If that sounds dismal, here is the good news: breakdowns can be *the* allies of accomplishment if they are seen not as problems but as opportunities for innovation and learning. When strategists meet barriers, they are not blocked but adapt quickly to the new circumstances. Breakdowns are the strategist's most underrated resource: If you analyze and harness them correctly—and the next section shows you what we consider the most powerful tool for doing so—they become raw material for break-throughs. A twenty-year study found that thirteen groundbreaking innovations, from Nike to Club Med, from Nautilus machines to Fed-Ex, from the Walkman to the VCR, from the CAT scanner to the Post-It, all arose like Phoenixes from the ashes of breakdowns when originally conceived.[117]

As long as you are at the strategy design stage, everything looks nice and tidy. But during strategy implementation, when the going gets tough, most of us fall into four traps. While each of them is only human and perfectly understandable, each is counterproductive.

Pitfall 1: Shame. Because we see breakdowns as negative, even shameful, we avoid giving bad news to superiors or colleagues. We keep it secret. Whether it is a failed client presentation, a faulty product, or being behind on a deadline, our instinct is to try fixing it before others ever find out. But how can you make good strategy when your people don't tell you the truth? The costs of hiding breakdowns can be huge. How could Bernard Madoff get away with his $50 billion Ponzi scheme for so long? The smart money knew Madoff was a crook because his returns were impossibly good. Nevertheless, when a rival money manager, Harry Markopolos, wrote to the SEC back in 1999 that "Madoff Securities is the world's largest Ponzi scheme," he was roundly ignored.

Pitfall 2: Blame. Breakdowns are inevitable stations on the strategy journey, but that's no consolation when they actually happen. They can make the best of us rip out our hair, chew our nails, or yell in uncontrollable rage at everyone around us. The smartest CEOs have been known to become utterly un-strategic, regress, and throw temper tantrums when the world seemed to turn against them. Jeffrey Skilling was so famous for his tongue-lashings that Enron employees were simply too afraid to tell him the truth. Even whistle-blower Sherron

Watkins expressed her concerns only anonymously—and she was one of the brave ones.

Despite a decade of shareholder activism, Enron is far from alone. Strategy teams or boards may resist bad news or people who rain on their parade. "I was never allowed to present to the board unless things were perfect," said a former Xerox executive about the company two decades ago (this has changed since then). "You could only go in with good news." Whoever gave bad news risked being blamed—or fired. The directors simply killed the messenger. And when they forced management to confront its poor performance, executives blamed short-term factors—from currency fluctuations to trouble in Latin America. This is the second pitfall when breakdowns happen: you blame yourself, your colleagues, or the game as a whole—"*I* am wrong, *they* are wrong, or *it* is wrong" ("it" being the task, the project, your job, or your entire organization). By the time then-president (and later CEO) Anne Mulcahy came out with the truth—the company had an "unsustainable business model," she told analysts in 2000—Xerox was already flirting with bankruptcy.

Pitfall 3: Hope. A survey of failed CEOs found a surprising commonality among them: instead of facing a breakdown head-on, *they simply wait.* "What is striking, as many CEOs told us, is that they usually know there's a problem; their inner voice is telling them, but they suppress it. Those around the CEO often recognize the problem first, but he isn't seeking information from multiple sources."[118] Everybody simply waits, hoping that the breakdown will somehow disappear and the brilliant strategy will take its rightful course. It probably won't. But often nothing happens, especially in organizations where people pass the buck. Even the people with whom the buck stops are not exempt from inaction and hoping. Worse, when CEOs feel threatened, "they focus even more on what brought them their success," said leadership guru Warren Bennis. "They dismiss anything that clashes with their beliefs." Such attachment to old solutions is, of course, the exact opposite of what would transform the breakdown into a breakthrough.

Pitfall 4: Hedge. The final, and perhaps most pernicious, pitfall is that you change (and usually lower) your strategic objectives instead of stretching to fill the gap. But your goals are far from being the problem; the commitment is in fact the solution. Whenever you commit to a strategic intent, you are bound to have a gap between present and future. In fact, breakdowns would not exist without background commitments. If you are not committed to anything, you will not have breakdowns—or accomplishments—of size.

The fact is, breakdowns are directly correlated to breakthroughs. When Pfizer tested Sildenafil, trials of the new heart medicine showed unwelcome and huge (forgive the pun) side-effects: male patients experienced increased blood flow to their penis. The drug enhanced the smooth muscle relaxant effects of nitric oxide, a chemical normally released in response to sexual stimulation.

·   If Pfizer managers had been ashamed, if they had conspired to keep the failure a secret, if they had done nothing and waited, or if they had wavered in their commitment to make a blockbuster drug, they would have preserved the status quo and lost the company lots of R&D money. Instead they made noise. They changed the small print about the unwelcome side effects into big print. They reframed and repackaged the medication as a lifestyle drug. To make a long story short, out of a breakdown—a malfunctioning heart medicine—a breakthrough was born. The new drug posted $1 billion sales in its first year and became a household name: Viagra.

So how do you turn breakdowns into breakthroughs? It's a three-step process:

Step 1: Declare a Breakdown. The first step is to make the breakdown public and interrupt business-as-usual. Your declaration of the breakdown forces you and your key stakeholders to confront the gap between current and desired performance. A breakdown in this context is not a thing; it is a speech act, a wake-up call that puts you back in the driver's seat. Churchill did this in the 1930s: while Germany re-armed and the British government appeased Hitler, he kept warning his compatriots of the Nazi threat—until he finally rose to prime minister at sixty-six, when most of us retire, and managed the breakthrough of vanquishing the German aggressor.

Step 2: Assert your Background Commitment. Keep in mind your underlying objective, without which there would be no gap. By declaring a breakdown, you serve public notice that it's unacceptable *in relation to a particular commitment*. Remember, and help others remember, why everyone committed to the goal in the first place. What would be missing in your organization, lives, or society if you gave up?

Step 3: Search for Options and declare the Breakthrough. Once you have declared the breakdown and recommitted your team to the original goal, the third step is to brainstorm new options for action. Don't be afraid to rattle people (and yourself) so they (and you) shift focus, think newly, and see opportunities previously not seen for filling the gap between status quo and desired result. One night several decades ago, when Philip Anschutz laid the groundwork for what was to become a multi-billion dollar fortune, he got a call. A drilling supervisor at one of his Wyoming oil rigs gave him the bad news: the well was on fire. And if the fire kept burning, it would bankrupt him.

Common-sense crisis management in such a case is to limit your exposure, sell off the bad investment and get out of there quickly. Anschutz did the exact opposite. He saw the bright side: the fire meant *he had finally struck oil*. He rented a plane, flew to Wyoming, and by 8:00 A.M. the next morning gambled more money on his oil venture—a lot more. He bought as much land around the burning well as he could. He hired Red Adair, a legendary oil-field firefighter, to put out the blaze, and invited a Hollywood studio to shoot the episode for the John Wayne thriller "Hellfighters." When he recalled the fire decades later, when he had become a billionaire, Anschutz said, "There's always a point that if you go forward you win, sometimes you win it all, and if you go back you lose everything."[119]

According to Churchill, "There are two types of people: those who see difficulty in every opportunity, and those who see opportunity in every difficulty." Strategy-In-Action needs the latter type.

Pitfalls in Phase 1: Shared Understanding

A senior manager from Dow Corning asked us in one of our workshops: "What if I open the floodgates and give my people permission to bring their ideas, but their ideas are stupid?" The manager was brave enough to voice a concern we see as a widespread reason why senior managers are reluctant to invite stakeholders to the strategy table. Similarly, the Strategy-In-Action sponsors at one global bank resisted the involvement of frontline managers or IT developers in the strategy process.

True, involving others may give license to extraneous or even counterproductive input, slow down decisions, tie up capacities unnecessarily, or simply waste time. But the payoff from deep ownership can be much greater than the cost. One solution is to come up with a cost-benefit analysis (what are the intended results, and how can you get these results with minimal input?); the other solution is to identify the frontline leaders, middle managers, and other stakeholders who can act as trendsetters or leaders at all levels of the organization. They are the ones who can represent their respective stakeholder groups, bundle smart input for the strategy, maximize ownership by their colleagues, and help keep the ship on course.

The Dow Corning manager above gave voice to another dirty thought that many senior managers are careful not to utter in public: "What if I empower people— and then they take over my job, and I lose my authority?" Knowledge is power, as the cliché goes. Many managers jealously guard their power and keep everybody else down and out of the loop. But in today's environment, such aloofness backfires. It's a vicious cycle: the farther your people are out of the loop, the more their actions will come out of left field, and the less you will want to involve them. On the other hand, the more involved they are, the more constructive their actions, the more strategic their results, the better they will make *you* look. And if one of them takes over your job, that will free you up to move on to greener pastures and greater leadership.

But even if those issues don't come into play, involving representatives of each key stakeholder group in the strategy process can be difficult. At one global bank, IT developers harbored intense mistrust against senior management, which had dragged its feet for too long, communicated badly, lost much credibility and was seen to work only for its own interests. What made matters worse was that the strategy sponsors did not want to invite any frontline people to the strategy sessions, so their input was never heard.

This was not the only problem. In our first strategy session with senior management, the executives in the room kept blaming the people who were not there (consistent with the French adage "Les absents on toujours tort," meaning the ones who are not there are always wrong), from the big boss to colleagues in other departments to frontline developers. Bad-mouthing ran freely. There was an unexpressed silo mentality, where the left hand had no idea what the right hand was doing, and where executives in one fiefdom within the company looked out mostly for their own interests and not for the whole company's. Nothing expressed these dysfunctions more than a briefing with senior managers, where one made no effort to hide his indifference by turning his back to the group, hunching over in his chair, and playing with his mobile during much of the session. Only when Thomas asked him to lead one of the breakout groups did the executive let go of his passive-aggressive posturing.

At a multinational energy company, we encountered another issue: In the pre-interviews before the start of the strategy process, some people were too intimidated to tell the truth. They were fearful for their jobs or afraid to antagonize their bosses. To get their unvarnished views, Thomas assured each stakeholder that the interviews were confidential, that we would come up with a blind summary that would integrate all responses and would hide who said what, and that the strategy sponsors were eager to hear what was really going on in the company and had promised not to penalize anyone for speaking up.

At yet another client, a die-cast manufacturer, the proverbial rhinoceros was lying right there on the table. It was a taboo in plain sight, and nobody wanted to talk about it. The presence of the CEO or another top manager with authority might—wittingly or unwittingly—hold people back from speaking up. We had to play devil's advocate and bring up several inconvenient topics that needed bringing up to get at a genuine shared understanding.

In these companies people spoke up too little, but at one medium-size company, people got so worked up that they fell into the opposite trap: some participants overpowered or ridiculed dissenting views. It was like an episode of "South Park." We had to make sure that all views got equal airtime, that people listened respectfully, and that those who went up against the group-think were not "excommunicated."

Pitfalls in Phase 2 : Strategic Intent

When the strategy team brainstorms the strategic intent, some people want to move on to the "how" too quickly, before the vision has enough room to breathe. Such premature concern for feasibility can kill the vision before it's even born. Skepticism has its place, but not at the strategic intent stage. For now, stakeholders must resist the temptation to evaluate ideas; all ideas are equally valid. Encourage participants to swing out, let it rip, and come up with wild ideas. The team can always edit out the stupid ones later.

A more harmful pitfall at the strategic intent stage is resignation. At one company, the defeatism was written all over people's faces. "Ah, here we go again. It's not as if we haven't warned them. I just know they'll fall on their noses again." Resignation can masquerade as realism, pessimism, or mere skepticism. It points to the past, not the future; and it has the power to kill off possibilities. So if resignation creeps into the process, you may first need to make sure all stakeholders let go of the past, then stay with the vision conversation until a future begins to live that goes beyond an extension of the past.[120]

Another pitfall is what happened at DaimlerChrysler, whose then-chairman Jürgen Schrempp had a vision for the joint company: "Das Beste oder Nichts" ("The Best or Nothing"). But despite the fact that Schrempp had touted DaimlerChrysler as a "merger of equals," Europeans dominated the combined entity from the start. Co-chairman Schrempp put himself firmly in charge and installed his trusted German aide Dieter Zetsche at Chrysler's helm. Schrempp refused an invitation by Chrysler's board to meet with them to build common ground and a joint future; instead he chose to go to his South African ranch. Because he had already thrown most Chrysler people off the joint management board—there were sixteen Germans and two Americans on the board—he could shove his vision down Chrysler's throat. But not for long. The company paid dearly for this new brand of German imperialism: soon it was forced to cut 28,000 jobs, its stock price tanked, and a decade later both DaimlerChrysler and Schrempp were history.[121]

DimlerChrysler is far from alone. At many companies, top managers have a vision that is not shared. You can be sure that people will be less productive when they don't own the company's strategic intent as theirs. At an Israeli military contractor, as one senior manager put it, the company president had "never explained to us his rationale, his motivation, what he wants and why." At a European space aviation contractor, the management board had even gone to great lengths to communicate its vision, but through lengthy PowerPoints that reduced the listeners to passive recipients. At one New York investment bank, Thomas asked a managing director for his vision, and he answered, "The CEO wants me to double revenue." That was the CEO's, not a shared vision. Thomas coached the executive in crafting a vision that was both inspiring to him and compatible with the company's overall strategy.

Pitfalls in Phase 3 : Indicators

The company might monitor the wrong metrics that fail to pull for the desired future or, worse, lead to unintended outcomes. For example, what indicators would pull for the right actions to end hunger and poverty?

Case: Metrics for Ending Poverty

THP found already in the 1980s that in the field of international development, development agencies used metrics for ending poverty like per-capita GDP or food production. While well-intentioned, these indicators were counter-productive—they made poverty even worse—because they pulled for the past instead of the future. Why? One fact is that hunger can be divided into two types: famines versus chronic hunger—or what the economist and Nobel laureate Amartya Sen called "endemic deprivation":

Famines are transient but violent events—they come and go, decimating the population and causing extreme misery and widespread death. In contrast, endemic deprivation is a more persistent phenomenon, forcing people to live regularly and ceaselessly in a state of undernourishment, disease and weakness. While endemic deprivation is less fierce as a calamity, it is also more resilient and affects more people. If famines kill millions through starvation and epidemic diseases, endemic deprivation can afflict hundreds of millions through debilitation and illness, increasing mortality rates and shortening people's lives.[122]

The UN Children's Fund (UNICEF), the World Health Organization (WHO) and THP all realized that they could not measure endemic deprivation (chronic poverty) with measurements of famines. They started using the infant mortality rate

(IMR), which measures the number of deaths among children (under age one) per 1,000 live births. Chronic hunger is said to persist as a society-wide condition in a country when that country's IMR lies above 50 per 1,000 live births.[123]

To produce a sustainable downward shift in infants dying, the quality of life of a vast majority of a society's inhabitants must improve. Hence, when we observe a sustained downward trend in the IMR, we can safely conclude that other social indicators have also improved. For example, available data indicate that a society's improvements resulting in a reduction of infant deaths simultaneously result in less child and adult deaths.[124] Infant mortality has proven to be a reliable indicator not only for babies' health, but also for nutrition quality and health of children and mothers, medical conditions, sanitary conditions of households, or the social status and rights of women and girls. Interviews in India and Bangladesh[125] suggest: when the IMR drops to 50 or below in a country (after a time lag of about five years), women begin spacing their births. Fertility drops because people realize that they need fewer children to insure themselves in old age.[126]

But even the IMR is not ideal. It measures desired outcomes and does not pull for the right actions that *give rise* to those outcomes. So THP started experimenting with metrics for action, given what is missing. It came up with the ratio of women leaders in business and society, or the percentage of girls in secondary education. You have to be creative, and you have to stand in the shoes of the implementers, or ask them: what actions do *they* need to measure for achieving the strategic intent?

Pitfalls in Phase 4: Thrusts

When Thomas worked with one of the world's largest cement manufacturers, we found that in the company's Houston operation, a recent acquisition, the newly installed Mexican boss had imposed objectives on his colleagues—or perhaps his superiors at headquarters had pushed the objectives on him, and he was simply passing on the pressure. Either way, his Houston colleagues never got to own the objectives as theirs, and unsurprisingly, merely pretended to give it their all for delivering.

Since the Mexican boss was unwilling to discuss a rationale for these objectives, let alone build a genuine shared understanding of all stakeholders, Thomas had to make do with what he had: he coached the executive vice president and his sales team to build their own objectives. The key was to build them such that they converged with the boss's key thrusts.

At a much smaller company, a military contractor, the problem was not that the objectives were imposed from above, but that there were simply too many of them. The company was seduced by a surplus of opportunities, and the board as well as top management failed to say "no" to loss-makers or cost-centers. This lack of focus drove everybody mad. The Danish philosopher Sören Kierkegaard said once, " Purity of the mind is to will one thing." Far better to do one thing well than three badly. At a Strategy-In-Action work session, the directors and top executives were brave enough to jettison the low performers.

Pitfalls in Phase 5 : Leadership and Culture

Leadership styles can clash, or cultures can clash. Both can hamper strategic alignment. At one global energy company, the boss failed to make his expectations clear, so few senior managers held themselves accountable for the objectives. At another, the president was so top-down that some managers who had worked there for ten years had yet to find themselves on the *floor* of his office, let alone inside it. If a manager was summoned to the inner sanctum, he or she would run the risk of being dressed down or scorned. The climate was one of fear and intimidation, which produced short-term results but not sustainable performance because executives were not intrinsically motivated. One day the boss had to fly to Budapest for a high-level meeting, but his flight was cancelled last minute while he was still at Hamburg airport. He took a taxi straight back from the airport shortly after 5pm—and was shocked to find virtually nobody at the office. To keep up appearances, they had stayed every day just until he left. It looked productive and was utterly unproductive.

To unleash leadership for the strategy, you have to get into the cultural mindset of people to see what makes them tick. In Kazakhstan, in a workshop for the government, the cabinet ministers in attendance were taciturn and evidently afraid to say the wrong thing and embarrass themselves in the eyes of the prime minister who was also in attendance. To unlock their participation, Thomas had to remind the participants that the word "Kazakh" meant originally something like "free citizen" or "free spirit." It worked, but not by luck alone: he could find the key in a flash of insight because he had done his homework to understand the target culture before he traveled there.

Ed worked with a technology company whose internet security product consisted of a back-office product and an appliance product. The company had been working on its next-generation converged product for almost three years when Ed joined to drive global expansion with the launch of their new product. The only problem: within weeks of joining the company, Ed found that the new product about to be launched was still years from completion.

The company operated two development centers, the back-office side in Seattle, Washington and the appliance side in San Jose, California. Far from compatible, the two products were so different that there was no way to integrate them. And the two engineering groups, primarily Taiwanese in San Jose, California and small-company Americans in Seattle, loathed each other's ideas, which obviously kept them from collaborating. The irony was that these were all good engineers. Nonetheless, Ed had to restructure engineering and brought in new leadership from outside because the existing team was dysfunctional enough to bring the company down with it.

At one Middle Eastern venture capital firm whose top managers Thomas coached on presenting the company's portfolio to American bankers and getting $100 million in additional financing, a heavy dose of machismo and stubbornness threatened to sabotage the process. The presenters were more committed to being right than to collaborating with American bankers or producing the result. At a dress rehearsal where two top managers showed a deck of PowerPoints, Thomas played devil's advocate: he threw in a bunch of questions to see whether the presenters could think on their feet. Instead of answering a question, one of them snapped, "Let me finish!" He did not deem it necessary to deal with challenges that would likely arise from American bankers. We had to coach them on being open to feedback, tackling questions diplomatically, and hearing questions as contributions instead of attacks.

To overcome such leadership or culture bindspots, the CEO and the top managers should invest in their self-awareness and cross-cultural competencies. It's a low-cost investment with a high return.

Pitfalls in Phase 6 : Catalytic Projects

In the Catalytic Project phase, which is really the launch of strategy implementation, some project teams run into a wall. At one global financial services firm, all participants in the Strategy-In-Action session got fired up and creative—until the conversation turned to allocating accountabilities for each of the seven catalytic projects they had designed. Suddenly it seemed like there was no time left over for this; each had too much on their plate. In an unspoken subtext, they all seemed to be saying, "Good luck with *your* project." One manager said it out loud: "So-and-so" (of course a colleague who happened to be out of the room at the time) "would be the perfect lead for this project." This temptation to pass the buck and shirk responsibility for action must be overcome head-on. We made it clear that each manager would lead or participate in at least one project, and we appointed one manager to coordinate the management of all projects.

Of course it can happen that people are at capacity with their existing duties, and really have no space for carrying out a catalytic project. If that is the case, the strategy team needs to free up time or capacity for the catalytic project and put certain other activities on the shelf if possible. What existing work could be canceled, postponed, or delegated to someone else to make room for the catalytic project? Something has to give; if a catalytic project shows up as extra work, then it needs to be better integrated with the strategic intent, or other activities should come under scrutiny to see if they are still needed for achieving the strategic intent.

At a military contractor we worked with, people fell into another trap: unclear promises and requests—or none at all. People tended to say, "We should..." or "They should..." instead of "I will..." or "I ask that you..." This happens often in meetings: people are reluctant to stick their neck out or talk straight to each other, or they are loath to take risks that might make them look bad if they fail. It might be useful to create a climate of straight talk in the team or company, encourage people to speak their minds and make clear promises and requests—with a clear action or deliverable, a clear deadline, and a clear recipient of the communication. Above all, during catalytic projects, make sure people communicate for action, which will cut out a lot of wasteful talk.[127]

Yet another possible pitfall is that executives suffer from focus anxiety; they are confused about what to do at any given moment, and when they do something they are consumed with worries about the opportunity cost of what they are not doing at that moment. Worse, people might encounter the close cousin of focus anxiety: a syndrome that our friend, the New York-based musician Marc Daine aptly calls the "Law of Infinite Prerequisites." The law works like this: In order to get something done, there is a prerequisite that would have to get done first; but getting that prerequisite done depends on a prior prerequisite; and so forth. To cut through such debilitating Gordian knots, you may have to coach people on setting clear priorities and putting them in a clear sequence.

Pitfalls in Phase 7 : Sustaining the Momentum

The moment people complete a 100-day catalytic project, they might rush on to the next thing and fail to reap any institutional learning from the project's success (or failure, as the case may be). But to speak with a military metaphor, consolidating the territory taken is just as important as planting the flag. Communicating a strategic success to enough of the right people—the frontline people, the stakeholders, the media—is at least as critical as the result itself. Jack Welch, the legendary former CEO of General Electric, was famous for spreading the word on any innovation he witnessed. Within hours of hearing a manager recount a highlight or best practice, he would send out a broadcast email to all GE employees around the world and share the learning with them.

Communication is crucial but not enough. In the aftermath of an intense catalytic project, people might lean back and rest on their laurels, they might fall into what the novelist John Updike once called "the twilight of inconsequence," or they might be confused or divided about where to go next. This is the time when the strategy team needs to be as vigilant as ever, take the pulse of the people, and intervene to sustain focus and momentum.

The Strategy-In-Action Worksheet

Now that we are coming to the end of the book, we thought it might be useful to sum up the Strategy-In-Action process in a simple worksheet (Table 10.1 below) you can use in your day-to-day at the office. The idea is that you (and the stakeholders of your choice) can see the entire strategy at a glance. (Tip: Start with the bottom and fill in the grid from bottom to top.)

Strategy-In-Action Worksheet			
(Anything else?)	6. Catalytic Projects?	7. Sustain Momentum?	(What could go wrong?)
2. Strategic Intent?	3. Key Indicators?	4. Thrusts?	5. Leaders? 5a. Gatekeepers?
1a. What's So Now?	1b. Missing?	1c. Blockages?	1d. Opportunities?

Table 10.1: Strategy-In-Action Worksheet

The Ten Commandments of Strategy-In-Action

We have distilled our experiences and best practices into a set of Ten Commandments of Strategy-In-Action. A manager cannot heed only some of these key success factors and discard others. No matter how good the strategy, sustained success happens only by juggling them all at once.

1. Leadership: Leaders are key but are often an afterthought for strategists. Above all the CEO and senior managers must engage personally and directly in the strategy and energize the organization toward goal attainment. Organizational leaders may need to change *themselves*—their assumptions, their attitudes, their behaviors—to lead by example. Without leaders who are willing to "be the change they wish to see in the world", to use Gandhi's phrase, the best strategy comes to naught.

2. People: Leaders unleash people power—human responsibility, creativity, and ingenuity. Strategy does not produce results; people do. But all too often people are received as recipients, not authors, of the strategy. Strategy-In-Action succeeds only when people make it happen. And the most innovative solutions might come from seemingly peripheral quarters, where people are less entrenched in the status quo than people at headquarters who may get a big payoff from keeping things just the way they are.

3. Ownership: People implement only what they own; to quote our colleagues Johnston and Bate again, people support what they help create. Leaders enable ownership of, and commitment to, the strategy by all stakeholders. They must ensure ongoing input to the strategy both top-down (from senior executives) and bottom-up (from implementers and end-users).

4. Partnership: Top-down leadership is out (except in crisis situations) and co-leadership is in. Collaborative leaders still have to make tough decisions alone, but if they get all perspectives first, they will likely make more grounded choices. Instead of hashing out plans behind closed doors, leaders maintain open and truthful communications and mutual trust between themselves and implementers, and address rumors and fears in the organization promptly and decisively.

5. *Value*: Any strategy must enhance the company's value or it is a waste of time. To maximize value to customers and end-users, shareholders and employees, leaders listen to the market and the customer so that the strategy process reflects the company's strategic environment. Listening beats trumpeting your value-add every time.

6. *Catalyst*: Rather than merely reacting to circumstances or crises, leaders generate change proactively. In addition to being strategists, they commit to playing a catalytic role. They are obsessed with achieving the strategic intent while being flexible about the means and pathways. They experiment with catalytic projects at low cost and low risk. No outcome is final: every outcome becomes a catalyst for further strategic action.

7. *Action*: Far from coming after strategy, action is both the driver of strategy and its supreme test. Leaders get continuous feedback from operational successes (*and* failures) and use it to reshape strategy. Strategy and execution make for an ongoing dialectic cycle of strategy-action-strategy-action-strategy, taking results and changes, feeding them back into the process, affecting changes in strategy, and so on. Any structure or infrastructure must support the strategy, not the other way around.

8. *Learning*: Leaders take risks and innovate. They celebrate successes and see failures as learning opportunities. They use breakdowns not as reasons for giving up or reducing their commitment, but as catalysts for breakthroughs. They hold the track record as "so what?" They focus on what's missing, on the obstacles and on opportunities for further integration.

9. Framing: Leaders are sense-makers. As new circumstances develop, they help all stakeholders make sense of the confusion and complexity by constantly adjusting the overall framework ("reframing"). They integrate the parts and look at the system as a whole, at the big picture.

10. Process: Leaders know that strategy is neither a plan nor an event. You can't check it off like just another item on a checklist. Strategy does not happen once; it becomes the framework in which everything happens. Strategy-In-Action is an attitude, a way of being and thinking that you integrate in your day-to-day work. "We want people to use these techniques daily in their work—using broad insights; learning faster; failing faster," says Cindy Tripp, marketing director at Procter & Gamble Global Design, about P&G's process that uses these principles. Needless to say, it's a new way of thinking for the $80+ billion global consumer products giant. Managers who have been with the company for many years describe P&G's former attitude about design as "the last decoration station on the way to market."[128] Needless to say, that has changed, and the company can never go back to the old ways. Such is the power of Strategy-In-Action.

~

Boiling It Down

❑ **Breakdowns are a natural part of the strategic process. You cannot have a dynamic strategy process without troubles; no accomplishment of size is possible, and life would be without spice. Indeed, breakdowns are often correlated to breakthroughs, and smart strategists make use of breakdowns to call forth breakthroughs, while avoiding the four pitfalls of shame, blame, hope, and hedge. The trick is to make the**

❑ breakdown public; revisit the background commitment; and search for options for the breakthrough.

❑ Derailers can happen at every stage of Strategy-In-Action, from building a shared understanding (phase 1) all the way to sustaining momentum (phase 7). This is particularly true for buy-in. Instead of taking it for granted or seeing it as a one-time event that can be checked off the list once and for all, strategists should see alignment as a process to manage. Buy-out (or pretend buy-in) can happen at every step of the process.

❑ The key success factors for Strategy-In-Action are ongoing top leadership commitment and involvement, unleashing people power, maximizing ownership, partnership with stakeholders, maximizing value, catalyzing change proactively instead of waiting until a crisis forces change, focusing on action and results, taking risks and innovating, framing and sense-making.

❑ Ultimately, Strategy-In-Action is not merely a business process; it is a way of life, a mindset, a way of doing business.

Further Reading

Andrews, Kenneth R. 1971. *The Concept of Corporate Strategy.* Homewood IL: Dow Jones-Irwin.

Ansoff, H. Igor. 1965. *Corporate Strategy: An Analytic Approach to Business Policy for Growth and Expansion.* New York: McGraw-Hill.

Argyris, Chris. 1991. "Teaching Smart People How to Learn," *Harvard Business Review*, May-June. 99-109.

Bossidy, Larry and Ram Charan. 2002. *Execution: The Discipline of Getting Things Done.* New York: Crown Business.

Collins, Jim. 1994. *Built to Last.* New York: Harper Business

_____. 2001. *Good to Great.* New York: HarperBusiness.

_____. 1999. "Turning Goals into Results: The Power of Catalytic Mechanisms," *Harvard Business Review*, July.

Drucker, Peter F. 2001. *The Essential Drucker.* New York: Harper Business.

_____. 1999. "Managing Oneself," *Harvard Business Review*, March-April. 65-74.

_____. 1988. "The Coming of the New Organization." *Harvard Business Review*, January-February. 45-53.

Eckerson, Wayne. 2005. *Performance Dashboards: Measuring, Monitoring and Managing Your Business.* New Jersey: Wiley.

Flaherty, James. 1999. *Coaching: Evoking Excellence in Others.* Boston: Butterworth-Heinemann.

Flores, Fernando, and Terry Winograd. 1986. *Understanding Computers and Cognition.* Norwood NJ: Ablex Publishing Corporation.

Goleman, Daniel. 1995. *Emotional Intelligence.* New York: Bantam Books.

_____. 2004. "What Makes a Leader?" *Harvard Business Review*, January 2004. 82-91.

Goodwin, Doris Kearns. 2006. *Team of Rivals: The Political Genius of Abraham Lincoln*. New York: Simon & Schuster.

Goshal, Sumantra and Christopher A. Bartlett. 1999. The Individualized Corporation: A Fundamentally New Approach to Management. New York: Harper Paperbacks.

Goss, Tracy, Richard Pascale, and Anthony Athos. 1993. "The Reinvention Roller Coaster: Risking the Present for a Powerful Future," *HBR* Reprint #93603.

Hamel, Gary. 1996. "Strategy as Revolution," *Harvard Business Review*, July-August. 69-82.

_____. 2002. *Leading the Revolution*. New York: Plume.

_____ and C.K. Prahalad. 1989. "Strategic Intent," *Harvard Business Review*, May-June. 63-76.

Handy, Charles. 1995. "Trust and the Virtual Organization," *Harvard Business Review*, May-June. 40-50.

Heidegger, Martin. 1968. *What Is Called Thinking?* Transl. by J. Glenn Gray. New York: Harper & Row.

Hofstede, Geert. 2001. *Culture's Consequences: Comparing Values, Behaviors, Institutions and Organizations Across Nations.* (2nd ed.) Thousand Oaks, CA: Sage Publications.

Katzenbach, Jon R. and Smith, Douglas K. 1993. *The Wisdom of Teams: Creating the High-Performance Organization.* Cambridge MA: Harvard Business School.Press.

Kotter, John P. 1990. *A Force for Change: How Leadership Differs from Management*. New York: Free Press.

_____ and James K. Leahy. 1993. "Changing the Culture at British Airways," Harvard Business School Case #9-419-009.

_____. 2007. "Leading Change: Why Transformation Efforts Fail," *Harvard Business Review*, January 2007.

Machiavelli, Niccoló. 1961. *The Prince*. London: Penguin Classics.

Miller, Robert and Stephen Heiman. 1986. *Strategic Selling*. New York: Warner Books.

_____. 1987. *Conceptual Selling*. New York: Warner Books.

Maturana, Humberto and Francisco Varela. 1987. *The Tree of Knowledge: The Biological Roots of Human Understanding*. Boston: Shambhala.

Moore, Jeffrey. 1991. *Crossing the Chasm*. New York: Harper Business.

_____. 1995. *Inside the Tornado*. New York: HarperBusiness.

_____. 1998. *The Gorilla Game*. New York: Harper Business

_____. 2000. *Living on the Fault Line*. New York: Harper Business.

Northouse, Peter G. 1997. *Leadership: Theory and Practice*. Thousand Oaks CA: Sage.

Parmenter, David. 2007. *Key Performance Indicators: Developing, Implementing and Using Winning KPIs*. New Jersey: Wiley.

Petersen, William G. 2002. *Reinventing Strategy*. New York: John Wiley & Sons.

Porter, Michael. 1985. *Competitive Advantage: Creating and Sustaining Superior Performance*. New York: The Free Press.

_____. 1986. *Competition in Global Industries*. Boston, MA: Harvard Business School Press.

_____. 1990. *The Competitive Advantage of Nations*. New York: The Free Press

_____. 1998. *Competitive Strategy: Techniques for Analyzing Industries and Competitors*. New York: Free Press.

_____ and Cynthia Montgomery (eds). 1979. *Strategy: Seeking and Securing Competitive* Advantage. Boston Massachusetts: A Harvard Business Review Book.

Prahalad, C.K. 2004. *The Fortune at the Bottom of the Pyramid*. Philadelphia: Wharton School Publishing.

_____ and Lieberthal. 1998. "The End of Corporate Imperialism," *Harvard Business Review*, July-August. 69-79.

Rahman, MD Anisur. 1993. *People's Self-Development: Perspectives on Participatory Action Research*. London: Zed Books.

Scherr, Allan L. 2005. "Managing for Breakthroughs in Productivity," Barbados Group Working Paper No. 1-05. Available at http://ssrn.com/abstract=655822

Schumpeter, Joseph A. *Capitalism, Socialism and Democracy*. New York: Harper.

Senge, Peter. 1990. "The Leader's New Work: Building Learning Organizations," *Sloan Management Review* (Fall), Reprint #3211.

Solomon, Robert C. and Fernando Flores. 2001. *Building Trust: In Business, Politics, Relationships, and Life*. Oxford: Oxford University Press.

Sun Tzu. [500 BCE] 1963. *The Art of War*. Translated and with an introduction by Samuel B. Griffith. London: Oxford University Press.

The Hunger Project. 1996. "Unleashing the Human Spirit: Principles and Methodology of The Hunger Project." New York: www.thp.org/reports/prin496.htm

Ulrich, Dave, Jack Zenger and Norman Smallwood. 1999. *Results-Based Leadership*. Boston, MA: Harvard Business School Press.

Weber, Max. "Bureaucracy" in *From Max Weber: Essays in Sociology*, H. H. Gerth and C. Wright Mills, eds. Oxford: Oxford University Press, 1946. Paper ed., 1958, pp. 196-244.

Weick, Karl E. 1996. "Drop Your Tools: An Allegory for Organizational Studies," *Administrative Science Quarterly*, 301-313.

Wineberg, Yosef, Sholom Wineberg and Levi Wineberg. 1998. *Lessons in Tanya*. Brooklyn: Merkos L'Inyonei Chinuch.

Zweifel, Thomas D. 2003. *Communicate or Die: Getting Results Through Speaking and Listening*. New York: SelectBooks.

_____. 2003. *Culture Clash: Managing the Global High-Performance Team*. New York: SelectBooks.

_____.2005. *International Organizations and Democracy: Accountability, Politics and Power*. Boulder CO: Lynne Rienner Publishers.

_____. 2010. *Leadership in 100 Days: A Systematic Self-Coaching Workbook*. New York: iHorizon.

_____ and Aaron L. Raskin. 2008. *The Rabbi and the CEO: The Ten Commandments for 21st Century Leaders*. New York: SelectBooks.

The Authors

Thomas D. Zweifel (thomas@thomaszweifel.com) is a management consultant, professor and author on strategy, leadership, and performance management. Since 1984 he has worked with top and senior managers in Fortune 500 companies, governments, UN agencies, and the military to design and implement strategies for breakthrough results. In 1997 he became the CEO of Swiss Consulting Group, which was named a "Fast Company" by *Fast Company* magazine and which he sold in 2013. Since 2000 he has taught leadership and Strategy-In-Action at Columbia University, St. Gallen University and other business schools in Israel, Switzerland, and the United States. Strategies based on his six books, including *Communicate or Die* (SelectBooks, 2003), *Culture Clash* (SelectBooks, 2003), *The Rabbi and the CEO* (SelectBooks, 2008, co-authored with Aaron L. Raskin), and *Leadership in 100 Days* (iHorizon, 2010) are used by 30+ Fortune 500 companies to maximize their return on people.

Born in Paris, Dr. Zweifel was educated in Switzerland and the United States, where he received his Ph.D. in international political economy from New York University. He is on the rosters of seven speaker bureaus and a frequent speaker in corporations and the media such as ABC, Bloomberg, CNN and *Financial Times*. In 1996 he realized his dream of breaking three hours in the New York City marathon, and in 1997 was "first finisher among CEO's who ran the New York City marathon" in the *Wall Street Journal*. After living in Basel, Berlin, Munich, Mumbai, London, San Francisco, Tokyo and New York from 1962 through 2008, he is now based in Zurich where he lives with his wife and their two daughters.

Edward J. Borey (edborey@frontier.com) is an experienced chairman, CEO and board member who has catalyzed growth and turnarounds in a half-dozen global companies, leading them from stagnation and heavy losses to profitability, sustainability and self-reliance. He is the past Chairman and CEO of WatchGuard Technologies (WGRD), the CEO of PSC (PSCX), and the COO of Intermec (UNA). Throughout his 37-year career, Ed served in a variety of executive positions in general management, marketing and finance for Global 1,000 companies. He began his turnaround work as a finance team member at Lear Siegler, turned around and built global department organizations for National Semiconductor and Pitney Bowes, as a general manager turned around and built The Retail Division of Monarch Marking, The Graphics Division of Paxar and the Media Division of Intermec. From there he moved to corporate leadership of publically held companies.

Currently, Ed serves on the Board of Arotech (ARTX). Prior public board experience includes WatchGuard (WGRD), PSC (PSCX) and MBrane (CNRT). To give back, Ed serves as a Board Member for the Northwest Chapter of the National Association of Corporate Directors and has served on the Snohomish County YMCA Board of Trustees. In 2010 Ed ran for the lower house of the Washington State Legislature. He received his B.S. in Political Science from State University of New York, College at Oswego; a Master of Arts in Public Administration from the University of Oklahoma; and an MBA from Santa Clara University. He lives in the Seattle area with his wife Susan.

More Books by Thomas D. Zweifel

Communicate or Die: Getting Results Through Speaking and Listening. New York: SelectBooks. (Also in Chinese, French, German, Indonesian)

Culture Clash 2: Managing the Global High-Performance Team. New York: SelectBooks. (Also in French)

Democratic Deficit? Institions and Regulation in the European Union, Switzerland and the United States. Lanham MD: Rowman & Littlefield.

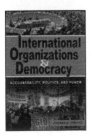

International Organizations and Democracy: Accountability, Politics, and Power. Boulder CO: Lynne Rienner Publishers.

The Rabbi and the CEO: The Ten Commandments for 21st Century Leaders. New York: SelectBooks. (2008 National Jewish Book Award and 2008 Foreword Book of the Year finalist; co-author Aaron L. Raskin; also in German, Polish, Russian)

Leadership in 100 Days: A Systematic Self-Coaching Workbook. New York/Zurich: iHorizon. www. thomaszweifel.com

Visit www.thomaszweifel.com for free excerpts, videos, tools, and more..

Strategy-In-Action Resources

If you are interested in applying this book to your company, visit www.thomaszweifel.com for books, tools, workshops, and processes that help companies and their leaders align on strategies, develop people power, and produce breakthroughs results:

Strategy-In-Action: a 7-step process of interviews leads to a shared understanding; a 2-day workshop aligns your management team around a bold business challenge and an elegant vision/strategy framework; and low-risk pilots pull the future to the present, yield quick wins and provide feedback to the strategy. Both Fortune 500 companies and mid-size companies have used this process to get organization-wide or inter-department alignment on their strategy and get quick wins toward achieving their vision. One global bank achieved cost savings of $200 million while boosting the morale of its 5,000 IT engineers; a top-tier energy company's retail team generated $74 million from innovative products and grew revenues by 11% while the industry lost 1%.

"The facilitator was excellent, the methodology great and the experience from working with other companies stimulating. I see measurable results in the organization: more (and more open) communication across managers and employees, better align-

ment across silos, and deeper ownership of the strategy. All three are essential for success."
—Dr. Mario Crameri, CIO Switzerland, Credit Suisse

Leadership-In-Action: a 2-day workshop provides leadership tools that last; systematically develops your high-potential leaders and fills their leadership gaps; and challenges their leadership in the action of meeting breakthrough goals through 100-day leadership projects. One Fortune 500 healthcare company used this service to enter the India and China markets with its diabetes diagnostic tool.

"We accomplished more than I would have even expected. This is being seen by the senior leadership as having the potential to shape how all of Johnson & Johnson does business."
—Sandra Thompson, VP Human Resources, Animas, a Johnson & Johnson Company

Coaching-In-Action: a 6-12 month process tailored to CEOs or senior executives fosters breakthroughs in their leadership ability in the action of meeting a business and/or leadership challenge.

"I wish I had had your tools 35 years ago when I was starting out."
—Werner Brandmayr, President, ConocoPhillips Europe

Communicate or Die: a 2-day workshop gives leaders tools for effective speaking *and* masterful listening in teams and/or organizations.

"... very good in the area in which I was most interested—building effective business relationships. I walked away with some tips for conduct as well as issues to keep in mind. Very helpful."
—Catherine Burton, Global Head Biostatistics, Novartis AG

Culture Clash: a 2-day workshop prepares leaders to avoid costly mistakes when working with or in other cultures (e.g. in virtual teams and/or outsourcing), and get the job done while respecting local values and customs.

"In my role ... it is paramount to cultivate a communication style that works across the globe in 23 different geographical and cultural regions. The workshop on Culture Clash was a very important step for me as well as my seniors. If we succeed in tapping into our vast pool of diversified skills and capabilities around the world and put them to work for our clients, UBS will have a bright future."
--Daniel Zweifel, Executive Director / Head Marketing Wealth Management, UBS

Notes

[1] William G. Petersen, "Strategic Learning: A Leadership Process for Creating and Implementing Breakthrough Strategies," Columbia Business School, 2001.

[2] Gary Hamel, "Strategy as Revolution," *Harvard Business Review*, July-August 1996, 69-82.

[3] Dietmar Hawranek, Martin Hesse, Alexander Jung, "A Generation of Uncertainty," *Der Spiegel*, December 31, 2012.

[4] Joann Lublin and Dana Matticoli, "Strategic Plans Lose Favor," *Wall Street Journal*, January 25, 2010.

[5] Lucio Cassia, Michael Fattore and Stefano Palleari, *Entrepreneurial Strategy: Emerging Businesses in Declining Industries*. Northampton MA: Edgar Elgar, 2006.

[6] Chris Hughes, Peter Thai Larsen and Haig Simonia, "Corroded to the core: How a staid Swiss bank let ambitions lead it into folly," *Financial Times*, April 21, 2008.

[7] James Surowiecki, "The Open Secret of Success," *The New Yorker*, May 12, 2008.

[8] Akio Toyoda, prepared testimony to the U.S. Congress Committee on Oversight and Government Reform, February 24, 2010.

[9] "U.S. Album Sales Down, Digital Sales Up," *Associated Press*, January 3, 2008; Apple press release, April 3, 2008.

[10] Nick Wingfield, "Nintendo Confronts a Changed Video Game World," *New York Times*, November 24, 2012.

[11] Tamar Levin, "College of Future Could Be Come One, Come All," *New York Times*, November 19, 2012.

[12] Kevin Done, "Air industry angst driven by oil and regulation," *Financial Times*, June 3, 2008.

[13] Chan Sue Ling and Liza Lin, "Airline Industry Will Take Three Years to Recover, IATA Says," *Bloomberg Business Week*, January 31, 2010.

[14] Molly McMillin, "Quality of Air Travel Sinks," *Wichita Eagle*, April 7, 2008.

[15] Kevin Done, "Air industry angst driven by oil and regulation," *Financial Times*, June 3, 2008.

[16] Michael Kunzelman, "BP has lost more than $100B in value since oil spill started," *Associated Press*, June 26, 2010.

[17] Sun Tzu, *The Art of War*. Harrisburg PA: Military Publishing Service Co. 1944.

[18] Niccoló Machiavelli, *The Prince*. London: Penguin [1514]1961). 90-91.

[19] Hans H. Gerth and C. Wright Mills, *From Max Weber: Essays in Sociology*. London: Routledge, 2007. Chapter 8, "Bureaucracy," 203-228.

[20] Frederick W. Taylor, "Report of a lecture by and questions put to F.W. Taylor: a transcript," *Journal of Management History*, 1:1, 1995. 8-32.

[21] Michael Walker, "Frequent Fliers," *Men's Vogue*, March 2008.

[22] BBC News, "One blog created 'every second'," August 2, 2005.

[23] Steve Hamm, "IBM vs. Tata: Who's more American?" *BusinessWeek*, May 14, 2008.

[24] Thomas D. Zweifel, *Culture Clash 2: Managing the Global High-Performance Team*. New York: SelectBooks, 2013. Revised edition.

[25] Chris Kanaracus, "Telecommuting: A Quarter of U.S. Workers Do It Regularly," *PC World*, November 28, 2007.

[26] *Harvard Business Review*, "Breakthrough Ideas for 2007."

[27] Eric von Hippel. *Democratizing Innovation*. Cambridge: MIT Press, 2005.

[28] Drucker, Peter. "Managing Oneself," *Harvard Business Review*, March-April 1999. 65-74.

[29] Henry Mintzberg, Bruce Ahlstrand and Joseph Lampel. *Strategy Safari: A Guided Tour Through the Wilds of Strategic Management*. New York: Free Press, 2005.

[30] Ashlee Vance, "Suit Over Faulty Computers Highlights Dell's Decline," *New York Times*, June 28, 2010.

[31] Martha Lagace, "What Really Drives Your Strategy? Q&A With Joseph Bower and Clark Gilbert," *Harvard Business School Working Knowledge*, January 9, 2006.

[32] Martha Lagace, *ibid.*

[33] Julie Salamon, "A Hollywood Used-to-Be Who'd Like to Be Again," New York Times, July 28, 2002.

[34] This account is based on Keenan Mayo and Peter Newcomb, "How the Web Was Won," *Vanity Fair*, July 2008.

[35] Interview by Keenan Mayo and Peter Newcomb, "How the Web Was Won," *Vanity Fair*, July 2008. 110.

[36] James Surowiecki, "The Return of Michael Porter," *Fortune*, February 1, 1999.

[37] Martha Lagace, "What Really Drives Your Strategy? Q&A With Joseph Bower and Clark Gilbert," *Harvard Business School Working Knowledge*, January 9, 2006.

[38] Joan Holmes, personal interview, New York City, January 26, 2008.

[39] Richard N. Haass, "Bill Clinton's Loose Organization," *New York Times* magazine, May 29, 1994.

[40] "How Procter & Gamble is using design thinking to crack difficult business problems," *Business Week*, July 30, 2008.

[41] Gretchen Morgenson, "Barbie's Guru Stumbles," *New York Times*, November 7, 1999.

[42] Dana Canedy, "Mattel Warns of Yet Another Profit Shortfall," *New York Times*, October 5, 1999.

[43] Gretchen Morgenson, "Barbie's Guru Stumbles," New York Times, November 7, 1999.

[44] Arjen van Ballegoyen, "Strategy-Oriented Management: Strategic Planning," seminar-training for the high-level Civil Service officials, Republic of Kazakhstan, Astana, April 25, 2008.

[45] Richard Rapaport, "To Build a Winning Team: An Interview with Head Coach Bill Walsh," *Harvard Business Review*, January 1993.

[46] Robert E. Johnston and J. Douglas Bate. *The Power of Strategy Innovation: A New Way of Linking Creativity and Strategic Planning to Discover Great Business Opportunities.* New York: Amacom, 2007. 85.

[47] See Thomas D. Zweifel, *Communicate or Die: Getting Results Through Speaking and Listening*, New York: SelectBooks, 2003.

[48] Carlos Ghosn, "Nissan Motor Co.: Directions for a Turnaround," interview, *Fast Company*, July 2002, 80.

[49] Joan Holmes, "The Hunger Project's Era 4," Title 2, Chapter 2, not dated.

[50] Michael Barone, "Detroit Automakers a Relic of the Past," *National Review Online*, November 1, 2008.

[51] Adrian J. Slywotzky and David J. Morrison (with Karl Weber), How Digital Is Your Business? New York: Random House 2001.

[52] Georgina Born, *Uncertain Vision: Birt, Dyke and the Reinvention of the BBC*. London: Secker & Warburg, 2004.

[53] Richard Sennett, *The Culture of the New Capitalism*. New Haven: Yale University Press, 2006. 56-57.

[54] Richard Foster and Sarah Kaplan, *Creative Destruction: Why Companies That Are Built to Last Underperform the Market—and How to Sucessfully Transform Them*. London: Financial Times/Prentice Hall, 2001.

[55] Michael Porter, *Competitive Strategy: Techniques for Analyzing Industries and Competitors*. New York: Free Press, 1998.

[56] Interview by Keenan Mayo and Peter Newcomb, "How the Web Was Won," *Vanity Fair*, July 2008. 106.

[57] Jon Gertner, "Capitalism to the Rescue," *New York Times* magazine, October 5, 2008.

[58] Amar Bhide, "How Entrepreneurs Craft Strategies That Work," *Harvard Business Review*, March-April 1994. 150-161.

[59] Gary Hamel, "Strategy as Revolution," *Harvard Business Review*, July-August 1996. 69-82.

[60] Gary Hamel and C.K. Prahalad, "Strategic Intent," *Harvard Business Review*, May-June 1989. 63-76.

[61] Hans R. Hinterhuber and Wolfgang Popp, "Are You a Strategist or Just a Manager?" *Harvard Business Review*, January-February 1992.

[62] Richard Rayner, "An Actual Internet Success Story," *The New York Times* magazine, June 9, 2002.

[63] Scott Brown, "An inquiry into the true volume of used book sales," *Fine Books & Collections*, May/June 2004. http://www.finebooksmagazine.com/issue/0204/used_books.phtml

[64] Fara Warner, "How Google Searches Itself," *Fast Company*, July 2002.

65 Della Bradshaw, "Academic on Quest to Harvest Top Ideas," *Financial Times*, October 22, 2007.

66 As part of the visioning process, participants may want to develop a tag line. Tag lines are often confused with the strategic vision and/or strategic intent; but each serves a different purpose. Strategic vision is the business' long-term "what" of the strategy; strategic intent is the strategic three-to-five year focus on the way to that vision; and a tag line is a sort of rallying cry of its purpose or intent. A tag line is necessary if the combination of the strategic vision and strategic intent leaves out a major component of the strategy that is important to make visible for customers, employees, and/or other stakeholders. For example, the tag line of Astrium, a satellite company that is a unit of EADS, is "Astrium, All the Space You Need."

67 C.K. Prahalad and Yves Doz, *The Multinational Mission: Balancing Local Demands and Global Vision.* New York: Free Press, 1987. 52.

68 Gregory G. Dess, G.T. Lumpkin, and Alan B. Eisner, "Nokia's Strategic Intent for the 21st Century," in *Strategic Management: Texts and Cases*, New York: McGraw-Hill, 2006. 751.

69 "Time to Cut Out Your Management Speak?" *Investors in People*, Issue 18, February 2007: 7.

70 Mohandas Gandhi, "A Note," *Mahatma*, VIII, 89, 8-47; cited in Richard L. Johnson (ed.), *Gandhi's Experiments With Truth: Essential Writings By and About Mahatma Gandhi*, Lanham MD: Lexington Books, 2005. 158.

71 Schwab, 1917, 39-41. Quoted by Werner Erhard et al., 2009, "A New Paradigm of Individual, Group, and Organizational Performance," Barbados Group Working Paper No. 09-02, 10 December, 30.

72 Jon Gertner, "Our Ratings, Ourselves," *New York Times* Magazine, April 10, 2005.

73 Gary Levin, "DVR viewers give a big boost to ratings for some shows," *USA Today*, June 19, 2009.

74 "Nokia Connects," *Bloomberg BusinessWeek*, March 27, 2006.

75 We owe this example to Arjen van Ballegoyen.

76 http://indexmundi.com/world/infant_mortality_rate.html

77 https://www.cia.gov/library/publications/the-world-factbook

[78] Joan Holmes, "Challenges for the Future of The Hunger Project: Presentation at the Global Board of Directors Meeting," April 22, 2007.

[79] Robert La Franco, "The Giant that Would Be King," *Red Herring*, August 15, 2001.

[80] Bloomberg, "Toyota Cites Driver Errors in Acceleration Cases," *Bloomberg Business Week*, July 14, 2010.

[81] Alex Taylor III, "Inside Honda's Brain," *Fortune*, March 7, 2008.

[82] Matthew E. May, *The Elegant Solution: Toyota's Formula for Mastering Innovation*. New York: Free Press, 2006.

[83] James Surowiecki, "The Open Secret of Success," *The New Yorker*, May 12, 2008.

[84] Interview in Nasdaq, "The Power of Collaborative Leadership," Advertorial, *Fortune Small Business*, September 2007.

[85] Tsun-yan Hsieh and Sara Yik, "Leadership as the starting point of strategy," *The McKinsey Quarterly*, 2005, Number 1, 67.

[86] Corporate University Xchange, "Leadership 2012," October 29, 2007. www.corpu.com/site_media/leadership/leadershipexecsummary.pdf

[87] Interview in Nasdaq, "The Power of Collaborative Leadership," Advertorial, *Fortune Small Business*, September 2007.

[88] David D. Kirkpatrick, "Executive's Role Stirs Rumors at Random House," *New York Times*, May 23, 2002.

[89] *Ibid.*

[90] The Hunger Project, "Basic principles of being on staff," unpublished manuscript, May 1993.

[91] David Nadler, presentation at 11th annual Wharton Leadership Conference, June 7, 2007.

[92] Cited in William G. Petersen, "Strategic Learning: A Leadership Process for Creating and Implementing Breakthrough Strategies," Columbia Business School, 2004.

[93] Jim Collins, "The secret of enduring success," *Fortune*, April 21, 2008.

[94] *Ibid.*

[95] Cited on Hotjobs.com website in 2000; Hotjobs was sold to Yahoo in 2002.

[96] Scott Kirsner, "Faster Company," *Fast Company* No. 34, May 2000. 162.

[97] Carlos Ghosn, "Nissan Motor Co.: Directions for a Turnaround," interview, *Fast Company*, July 2002, 80.

[98] Interview with R. Buckminster Fuller, *Playboy*, February 1972.

[99] James Bennet, "The Radical Bean Counter," *New York Times Magaazine*, May 25, 2003.

[100] Donald N. Sull, Alejandro Ruelas-Gossi, and Martin Escobari, "Innovating Around Obstacles," *Strategy & Innovation*, November-December 2003, 12-15.

[101] www.developmentmarketplace.org

[102] Robert C. Wood and Gary Hamel. "The World Bank's Innovation Market," *Harvard Business Review*, November 2002. 104-113.

[103] The Hunger Project, http://www.thp.org/what_we_do/key_initiatives/community_centers/overview.

[104] "Nokia Connects," *Bloomberg BusinessWeek*, March 27, 2006.

[105] Eric McNulty, "Robert Sutton: How to balance strategy development and implementation," *Strategy & Innovation*, November-December 2003. 16.

[106] Tom McNichol, "A Startup's Best Friend? Failure," *Fortune Small Business*, April 2007.

[107] "Citizenship in a Republic," speech at the Sorbonne, Paris, April 23, 1910.

[108] Gary Hamel and C.K. Prahalad, "Strategic Intent," *Harvard Business Review*, May-June 1989. 63-76.

[109] The term was popularized by Mark Twain, who attributed it to the British prime minister Benjamin Disraeli, but the most plausible source is Charles W. Dilke, who "was saying the other day that false statements might be arranged according to their degree under three heads, fibs, lies, and statistics." *The Bristol Mercury and Daily Post*, October 19, 1891.

[110] Katherine Kane, "From Operating Action to Strategic Action: MDS's Scorecard Journey; An Interview with Robert B. Harris, Senior Vice President of Strategy, MDS," Balanced Scorecard Report, Harvard Business School Publishing 5:6, November-December 2003, 9.

[111] Ron Ashkenas, "Simplicity-Minded Management," *Harvard Business Review*, December 2007, 101-109.

[112] "Scale-Up: The Next Great Challenge," The Hunger Project, October 2006; "Scaling Up What Works," The Hunger Project, March 2007; Epicenters in Africa: Five Years to Self-Reliance," The Hunger Project, October 2007; "President's Report to the Global Board of Directors, " April 2009, www.thp.org/learn_more/speeches_reports/reports/presidents_report_april_2009.

[113] The Hunger Project, "Uganda: Positive External Assessment and Improving Health Resources," Update to the Global Board, April 2009. http://www.thp.org/learn_more/news/latest_news/uganda_april_2009_update_to_global_board

[114] David C. Korten, "Strategic Organization for People-Centered Development," *Public Administration Review* 44:4, July-August 1984, 341-352.

[115] Venkatesh Rao, "Why Amazon Is the Best Strategic Player in Tech," *Forbes*, December 14, 2011.

[116] ibid.

[117] P.Ranganath Nayak and John M. Ketteringham. *Breakthroughs!* New York: Rawson Associates, 1986. 347.

[118] Ram Charan and Geoffrey Colvin, "Why CEOs Fail," *Fortune*, June 21, 1999.

[119] Graham Bowley, "Goal! He Spends It on Beckham," *New York Times*, April 22, 2007. BU1.

[120] See Thomas D. Zweifel, *Leadership in 100 Days: A Systematic Self-Coaching Workbook*, New York: iHorizon, 2010. www.thomaszweifel.com.

[121] See Thomas D. Zweifel, *Culture Clash: Managing the Global High-Performance Team*, New York: SelectBooks, 2003. 33.

[122] Amartya Sen, "Public Action to Remedy Hunger," Fourth Annual Arturo Tanco Memorial Lecture. London: The Hunger Project, 1990. 7.

[123] Population Reference Bureau, *World Population Data Sheet*. Washington, DC: Population Reference Bureau 1983.

[124] The Hunger Project. *Ending Hunger: An Idea Whose Time Has Come*. New York: Praeger Publishers, 1985. 384.

[125] The Hunger Project. *Ending Hunger Briefing*. New York: The Hunger Project, 1985.

[126] Thomas D. Zweifel and Patricio Navia, "Democracy, Dictatorship, and Infant Mortality," Journal of Democracy 11:2, April 2000. 99-114.

[127] See Thomas D. Zweifel, *Communicate or Die: Getting Results Through Speaking and Listening*. New York: SelectBooks, 2003.

[128] "How Procter & Gamble is using design thinking to crack difficult business problems," *Business Week*, July 30, 2008.

Index

NBC, 91-92
Netherlands, 42
Nongovernmental organization (NGO), 45, 153
Nielsen, 89-91
Nokia, 2, 71, 78-79, 81, 93-94, 156-157, 163
Novartis, 2, 16, 115, 215
Nucor, 2, 139

O
Odland, Steve, 1
Office Depot, 1
Ownership, 55, 60, 77, 80-81, 86, 104, 186, 198, 214
O'Neal, Stanley, 135

P
Palestinian Authority, 150
People-centered, 30, 37
Performance, 59, 81, 88, 94, 99-100, 104-108, 117, 127, 135, 141, 154, 160, 170-171, 173, 183-184, 192, 209, 211
Pfizer, 184
Porter, Michael, xii, 17, 28, 31, 58
Prahalad, C.K., xii, 28, 31, 71, 78-80, 162
Proof-of-principle projects, 36, 150, 159

Q
Quick wins, xvii, 149, 153, 157, 159, 213
QWERTY keyboard, 70

R
Random House, 19, 132
Return on Investment (ROI), 12, 80, 82, 133
Roosevelt, Franklin D., 32
Roosevelt, Theodore, 27, 37, 158

Made in the USA
Middletown, DE
16 February 2022